COUNTRY STORES
OF
VERMONT

COUNTRY STORES
OF
VERMONT

A HISTORY AND GUIDE

DENNIS BATHORY-KITSZ

Charleston   London

THE
History
PRESS

Published by The History Press
Charleston, SC 29403
www.historypress.net

Unless otherwise noted, all images are courtesy of the author.

First published 2008

Manufactured in the United Kingdom

ISBN 978.1.59629.475.2

Library of Congress Cataloging-in-Publication Data

Báthory-Kitsz, Dennis, 1949-
A guide to the historic country stores of Vermont / Dennis Bathory-Kitsz.
p. cm.
Includes bibliographical references and index.
ISBN 978-1-59629-475-2
1. General stores--Vermont--History. 2. Retail trade--Vermont--History.
I. Title.
HF5429.4.V4B28 2008
381'.109743--dc22
                    2008021045

Notice: The information in this book is true and complete to the best of our knowledge. It is offered without guarantee on the part of the author or The History Press. The author and The History Press disclaim all liability in connection with the use of this book.

For Gene Morel
the quintessential Vermonter who knew the meaning of curiosity, honesty and humor
—and taught the rest of us

Contents

Contents

PREFACE

When I crossed into Vermont some thirty years ago—part of the last northward urban exodus of the twentieth century—the clouds seemed low and elusive, almost a fog just above my eyes. They appeared and vanished as my headlights shone into the unlit darkness of Interstate 91. This mystery continued for miles until its distracting flicker forced me to stop on the shoulder to investigate the evanescence.

These ghosts were not clouds. They were Northern Lights—the first time in my then thirty years that I had seen them, having lived only in the hazy skies downcountry. It was a welcome sign of a new time of clarity and illumination—although the societal welcome into Vermont wasn't what I expected.

The Dutch use the word *allochtoon*. If you were born outside the Netherlands, you're one. If either parent was born outside, you're still one. Only the third generation lifts the approbation of *allochtoon*. They're known as flatlanders in Vermont—even those "flatlanders" from the towering Rockies. But a flatlander family must stay here longer than a mere three generations. I know that because within my first month in Vermont, I was told this story:

In an unpainted Adirondack chair on the country store porch sat a white-bearded man, old & ageless, feet flat down, stiff as carved wood, unlit pipe gently massaged between his teeth. Mud season had yielded its morass into firm summer, and a recent arrival who had settled into the hills drew up a neighborly chair. "It feels good to be a Vermonter," he said with a deep, satisfied, downcountry-accented sigh. The old man stared hard ahead past the lad's hopeful look. The pipe scarcely moved as he said, "Not a Vermonter. Never be a Vermonter." The next year, after the younger man's first winter, the same conversation began and ended the same way. A decade later, the not-so-much-younger man—married and work-worn—engaged again in the discouraging exchange on the porch as noticeably more cars drove by than in past years. Always the flatlander he'd be, it seemed. More years fell from the calendar, but this time the younger man, his beard now tinged with its own aging gray, rushed up with a wide grin. "Well, now, old friend. We've just had a baby. I will never be a Vermonter—but my daughter is a Vermonter!" He waited. The old man's expression cracked a whitetail's flick, then settled back into incorrigibility. Still staring straight ahead through the haze of years, he admonished, "Cat climb into the oven to have kittens, it don't make 'em muffins."

Now *that's* Vermont, and it explains the survival of this tough little state and its farmers and merchants. Years-long dramas like that above unfold slowly, every day, on the front steps of the country stores.

ACKNOWLEDGEMENTS

The history of Vermont's country stores cannot be told in a single volume, or in a dozen. It is the story of individual storekeepers and individual communities in the once and present most rural state of the union. With its 251 towns, each at one time with perhaps two or three country stores, and a history that includes agriculture, quarrying, technology and tourism, Vermont's store tales *are* its stories.

To the storekeepers who do not see their carefully tended enterprises here, I say: Tell your own story now before it is lost in the mists of time. Like the Tschorns of the Wayside in West Arlington or the Billingses of F.H. Gillingham's in Woodstock, put down your recollections, collect the photos and unearth the clippings. The story must be told. Tell it.

My sincere thanks to my wife Stevie Balch for her encouragement to get involved with Vermont's country stores, and to all who contributed to this slim volume. Among them are the dedicated storekeepers Marilyn Bellemare,

ACKNOWLEDGEMENTS

Machs' General Store, Pawlet; Jireh Billings and Frank Billings, F.H. Gillingham's, Woodstock; Billy Browlee, H.N. Williams, Dorset; James Currier, Currier's Quality Market, Glover; Rick Dente, Dente's Market, Barre; Doug Edwards, Buxton's Store, Orwell; Jan and Al Floyd, Floyd's Store, Randolph Center; Dan Fraser, Dan & Whit's, Norwich; Jody Fried and Becky Daley, Bailey's & Burke, East Burke; Will Gilman, Will's Store, Chelsea; Jay Hathaway, formerly of Peltier's Market, Dorset; Jane Hastings Larrabee and Jenny Larrabee Rafuse, Hastings Store, West Danville; Chief Lone Cloud, Evansville Trading Post, Brownsville; Bill MacDonald, Waits River General Store; Janet MacLeod, Adamant Co-Op; Andy Mégroz, Panton General Store; John Rehlen, Castleton Village Store; Jon St. Amour, Jericho Center Country Store; Nancy and Doug Tschorn, Wayside Country Store, West Arlington; Randy Whitney, Roxbury Country Store; Charlie Wilson, Taftsville Country Store.

Special thanks to publisher Robert "Dike" Blair of Middlebury for permission to use Walter Hard's poetry from *A Mountain Township*, and to David Budbill for permission to include an excerpt from *Judevine*.

Appreciation to those who provided expertise, information, assistance and tales of country stores, including Jim Harrison, Vermont Grocers' Association; Gary Lord, Brookfield Historical Society; Kay Schlueter, Northfield Historical Society; Barbara Parker and Don Sherefkin, Marlboro Historical Society; Wilhelmina

Smith, Greensboro Historical Society; Charlotte Downes and George Hayes, East Burke Public Library; Kevin Graffagnino and Bob Murphy, Vermont Historical Society; Shannon Bedor, Northeastern Vermont Development Association; Reenie de Geus, Vermont Department of Agriculture; Johnathan Croft, VTrans Mapping Unit; Gregory Sanford, Vermont state archivist; Hans Raum, Vermont Collection curator, Middlebury College; Bert Sargent, Jiffy Mart, New Haven; Wally Aseltine, Northfield; Bill Keogh, Burlington; Wesley Chandler, Benson; William Harris, Shoreham; Jayne Nold-Laurendeau, Northfield Falls; Raymond Smith, West Arlington; Ross Warren, Dorset; and Pantah, MZcountryboy, hahv, Boondox and bitterjoe of Adventure Rider Motorcycle Forums.

Thanks also to Janet Long, Greensboro Historical Society; Keith P. McCusker, Betty Irons and Wendy Cox, Norwich University; Greg Gerdel, Vermont Department of Tourism and Marketing; Mark Favreau, Favreau Graphic Design; Michael Lynch, Middlebury College Library; the employees of Barnard General Store, Jericho Center General Store, Lisai's Market, Machs' General Store, Panton Store, Taftsville Store, Willey's Store and H.N. Williams Store.

And of course thanks to my editor and disciplinarian, Rachel Roesler of The History Press.

PART I

The History of Vermont's Independent Country Stores

THE SPINE OF
THE GREEN MOUNTAINS
GEOGRAPHY AND SPIRIT

My father ran the country store. He was successful; he trusted nearly
everybody, but lost a surprisingly small amount. He knew how to lay
bricks and was an excellent stone mason. The lines he laid out were
true and straight, and the curves regular. The work he did endured.
—Calvin Coolidge

The Early Days

The musty country store is a reminder of Vermont's quaint,
kinder, gentler past—a Norman Rockwell painting on the cover
of a travel brochure. But that past is an illusion. Vermont's past
was neither gentle nor kind, and we are never quaint in our own
times. No, the country store is the modern heritage of a tough,
independent past. And the country stores live on, musty smell
and all—hundreds of them, plain or cluttered or historical or
touristic, in the centers of Vermont's 251 towns and villages.

The history of country stores is deeply intertwined with life in Vermont. Where there were roads, there came stores. Farmers, stores. Railroads, stores. Local needs, stores. Tourists, stores. It is a village culture, and villages ultimately give life to these stores. The land that became Vermont was once a green and mountainous wilderness, with a deep canopy of winter snow that lasted from November to May. A few settlements by Lake Champlain were founded in the 1660s, Fort Dummer was built in 1724 and a trading post appeared by 1731 at the French settlement at Chimney Point.

Vermont's eventual political borders were chiseled from the tussle between the colonies of New York to the west and New Hampshire to the east, with some southward pulling by Massachusetts. Vermont saw its first town of Windsor granted a charter in 1772, and it lived briefly as an independent republic (with its own money) before joining the union in 1791. Largely made up of random patches of settlers and occasional aboriginal nomads such as the Abenaki—for whom the territory was little more hospitable for year-round living than it is today, and who preferred the Champlain Valley, Lake Memphremagog and the grassy Coos near Newbury in the Connecticut River Valley—Vermont slowly saw its hilltops and wide river valleys settled with farmers and self-sufficient tradespeople. The Abenaki continued to plant, fish and hunt as the seasons allowed.

Despite its remoteness, most of Vermont was settled before statehood. The earliest settlements—those before

1768, when 138 townships were granted to colonists by New Hampshire—began in the two-thirds of the Connecticut River Valley bordering New Hampshire to the east, and the southwest corner including Bennington, where the lush Taconic and Champlain Valleys joined. Settlement grew rapidly after the French and Indian War in 1764. Settlers came from Connecticut, Massachusetts and Rhode Island, bringing their families and building the Congregational churches that still dot the landscape.

By the American Revolution, settlers had expanded inland along the rivers that could provide power to sawmills and northward along Lake Champlain to plant crops, following the path of defensive military positions and also making their way along the Bayley-Hazen Military Road from the Connecticut River to the state's wild northern interior. In the following decade, all the river valleys were being busily settled except for those in the far northeast and the unwelcoming spine of the Green Mountains. After 1791, what is now the ski country near Warren and north of Stowe, along with the remote Northeast Kingdom, finally saw settlers willing to brave the elements.

By 1795, the new Vermont Legislature began authorizing turnpikes in the long, spiny state. Vermont runs 261 miles from the Canadian border to Massachusetts, and within its 9,250 square miles of land exist 251 named towns—including one with no population at all—and some 300 country stores. Its climate is similar to Minsk, Stockholm and Fargo—not, as even today's newcomers discover, full of welcoming charm and pastoral recreation save for a few summer months. Its Green Mountains are part of the Appalachian chain, with the highest peak Mount Mansfield, at 4,393 feet. It is filled with streams and lakes, fertile valleys along Lake Champlain to the west and the Connecticut River to the east, stretches of dense forest that once dominated the entire region, hardscrabble farming land and a brittle spine of mountains that divides geography and politics—a divide that from Vermont's early days into the mid-twentieth century followed "mountain rule": the two-year governorship and state power alternated between east and west, seeing to the interests of the entire land.

Vermont's early days were times of barter. Isolated by the Green Mountains, long winters—nine months of denuded trees and snow-covered landscape—and few roads, farmers traded milk, mutton, fur and wood. Traders came through. Farms failed. People grew sick. It wasn't charming. It was desperately hard work.

Once Vermont was politically stable and its population started to grow, itinerant peddlers began bringing up supplies and manufactured goods from commerce centers and nascent mill towns to the south, and then settling into communities as the growing towns could support them. Supplies traveled easily by boat, and with greater difficulty by road. The peddlers could keep their purchasing contacts downcountry and use local supplies (building wood from sawmills and grains from gristmills) in trade. Along with the tavern and the church, there grew to be two general stores in most towns—one for the farm with feed and machinery, and one for the home with groceries and fabric.

Vermont's story is one of individualism. Farms and mills, each different, were defined by lowlands, hills, river bends and seasons. Unlike the distinct towns and farms of southern New England, Vermont was a story of loose-knit communities, freedom and independence, unshackled by Puritan culture.

Country and general store owners were hardworking and serious. Storekeepers stand in front of their newly opened store in Greensboro. *Courtesy Greensboro Historical Society.*

From the beginning, contrary to the popular image of a backwoods culture, literacy was high—greater than in the United States as a whole. Indeed, Castleton College was chartered in 1787, four years before Vermont became a state. One-room schoolhouses were nestled into the landscape of every town and village well into the late twentieth century. By 1900, only Maine had lower illiteracy than Vermont's 6.4 percent, and Vermont continued as one of the most literate New England states through the 1960s (when statistics were discontinued), dropping to the region's lowest at 1.1 percent.

Perseverance was as high as literacy; farms and businesses were established for the long term, starting on hillsides. The general store in Jericho Center—the "center" towns are most often in the hills—opened its doors in 1808 and has never closed. According to Charles Morrissey in *Vermont: A History*, a "hillside mentality" made sense for Vermont.

The early settlers first cleared the upper slopes because morning fog tended to envelop the valleys in white cocoons while the uplands were basking in sunlight. After heavy storms, the valleys were more likely to be flooded, and in hot spells which spawned mosquitoes the danger of sickness seemed greater. In the winters the valleys often were colder than the hilltops because, as every Vermonter knows, cold air is heavier than warm air and can bring frosts to the lowlands while the highlands are spared.

A knowledge of the land brought progress and the regional economy was growing from Boston to the Canadian border. Farmers in Vermont learned the land and began to have surplus goods to sell. They needed cash and barter, but cash wanted to be spent. So with the movement of goods and new turnpikes, there were supplies to buy and the need to find a place to buy them. Well-developed Rutland had shops by 1788, and the first commercial villages appeared in Middlebury and Springfield in 1790.

Soon the typical Vermont village was born.

Village and Forest

In Abby Hemenway's monumental *Gazetteer*, Elmore, a typical Vermont town of the mid-nineteenth century, is described: "There is a small village in the north-western part of the town, at the outlet of Elmore pond, consisting of about a dozen dwelling-houses, one hotel, one store and grocery, a harness-shop, a carriage-shop, which does an extensive business, a post-office, starch-factory, blacksmith shop, with church and school."

On the other hand, nearby East Elmore was built upon the lumber industry, but with forests depleted by the early twentieth century, the industry—and the town—disappeared. East Elmore had a general store, post office, mills, homes and its own school…and now was gone. Elmore itself is now a scenic town on the banks of Lake Elmore with a thriving country store, state forest, hiking trails and a fire watchtower.

The forests that blanketed Vermont also kept it productive and warm—though the toll on the forests was high through the nineteenth century. The first documented clearing was by Samuel Robinson in 1761 in Bennington, to build the East Bennington sawmill and then a gristmill. Cutting of trees began in earnest. Sawmills made boards for roads, bark, "treen" (sturdy ammunition boxes and shipping crates), barrels, willow for baskets and other wickerware and boards for home heating of what were ultimately thousands of farmhouses, for charcoal and later in the century for burning in locomotives.

A cord is roughly 128 cubic feet, with each tree contributing about 60 percent of a cord, with the rest of the tree scrub. Locomotives traveled twelve miles per cord. The cost to trees of a single long run was staggering. Traveling the length of Vermont round trip would consume *forty-four* cords of wood—about seventy trees per round trip. The vitality of the rail system was so enormous that if the schedule had one daily run from border to border—and there were far more (and less efficient) than that, especially when hauling marble and granite—more than twenty-five thousand trees vanished *per train* each year.

Vermont mills made treen until the shipping of milled lumber out of state grew dramatically. Lumber shipped from

Burlington increased through the years from 1860, reaching a peak of 375 million board feet in 1889. From early clearings in the forest through nineteenth-century lumber markets to the state's nearly thirty-six thousand farms in the 1880s, the hillsides were devastated, and the soil was exposed and eroded during snow melt. With the forests being cleared for fuel for trains and plank roads, as well as by the sheep craze of the 1830s, the forests did not begin to recover until the century's end.

So the virgin forests were felled. What were they like? Early accounts abound, but at H.N. Williams's store in Dorset, originally a carriage shop, one can see the reality of those virgin boards in the attic. The roof, protected by shingles of local slate—another Vermont resource—is made of boards twenty-two inches wide, cut in 1840 when the store was new and the forests were still standing. By century's end, the hillsides and valleys were cleared, the virgin forests were gone and up to 75 percent of the state had become pasture, homes and towns. It was the abandonment of sheep farming, the decline of the railroads and the slowing growth that brought the forests back. Forests today cover 75 percent of the state, and the present forests provide the sugarbush—groves of tappable maple trees.

The common product in every country and general store in Vermont is maple syrup, and in fact a hefty 37 percent of national production comes from Vermont's trees. It takes four trees to produce the forty gallons of sap needed

Twenty-two-inch virgin pine boards at H.N. Williams Store in Dorset, protected for 170 years under cover of a well-maintained local slate roof.

to make a gallon of syrup, and in March when nights drop below freezing and days are beginning to warm, the steam and wood smoke rising from evaporators in sugarhouses announce that sugaring season is underway. Ward Knapp recalls the average sugarbush was fifteen hundred tapped trees, and even today family members relieve each other to keep the evaporators going, whether they are fed from zinc-plated buckets carried in from the sugarbush or a web of PVC pipe that gathers drops into trickles and trickles into rivers of sap that flood into evaporator pans.

Sugaring in West Arlington, circa 1950. Teams of horses are still occasionally used to collect cans of sap in areas of sugarbush, but some modern farmers use a web of PVC pipe. *Courtesy Nancy Tschorn, West Arlington.*

The early sap is the clearest, resulting in the fancy grades of Vermont syrup. But for a true taste of what Vermonters use, find Grade B or even a private stock of industrial-grade maple syrup—a thick, dark brown syrup that's called "sticks and twigs." It's not for the faint-tongued.

The Morgan Horse and the Sheep Craze

Rural agriculture can produce surprises, one of which was Figure, a horse purchased by Randolph Center musician and schoolteacher Justin Morgan. Brought to Vermont in the 1790s from Morgan's hometown of West Springfield, Massachusetts, Figure had a compact physique and temperament suited to Vermont's climate and agricultural needs. It was a genetic mutation, and Morgan recognized it. The breed is sometimes called "a pony in horse size," but without pony behavior, and with an exceptional temperament and willingness to work with intractable owners. Sturdy above all, resistant to illness, needing very little feed or upkeep, curious, trusting, very strong, Vermont's Morgan is more versatile than most horses—fleet, and while on the smaller side, able to carry an adult all day. The even-tempered, hardworking Morgan spread from Vermont elsewhere, from plow horse and cart horse and trotter to service in the Civil War, ultimately designated Vermont's state animal in 1961.

As for Justin Morgan himself, his music fell into obscurity until the mid-twentieth century, when a revival of early American music revealed the brilliance of such compositions as "Amanda," a hymn written on the death of his infant daughter and later frequently performed (under this author's direction) at the Union Congregational Church a few hundred feet from Roxbury Country Store. Justin Morgan's

Country stores are open every day, all day. The flag flies in front of Floyd's Store in Randolph Center after another snowfall in the winter of 2008.

homestead is on Fish Hill Road, and he is buried near Floyd's Store in Randolph Center.

Giving shape to Vermont's hills in the nineteenth century was the sheep craze. It is hard to imagine the extent and length of this madness, which rivaled the great "Tulip Mania" in the Netherlands, when a single bulb could sell for 6,000 florins. It began when William Jarvis, the American consul to Lisbon, sent a flock of Portuguese Merino sheep to Weathersfield in 1811. By 1840, there were close to 1.7 million sheep in Vermont, grazing on every blade of grass in the increasingly cleared pastures—and there grew country stores to match, with Bridgewater Corners, Dorset, Newbury, Taftsville, East Calais, Middlesex, Randolph Center and Chester building stores within ten years.

Vermont was covered in sheep. Addison County produced the greatest wool per acre in the United States. Breeding was rampant, farms expanded and small subsistence farmers were bought out and left Vermont. Mills in New England, most of them downcountry, were meeting the needs of 50 percent of the wool and 80 percent of the cotton goods in the United States. Vermont's mills were bursting at the seams during the sheep craze, and picked up the substantial overflow from the South.

And then it happened: tariffs were lowered in 1841 and imported wool began to compete with that from Vermont, and the newly laid railroads brought cheap wool from the West. Flocks were slaughtered—more than half of all the sheep in Vermont—by 1850. But the damage was done. Forests had been cut for pasture and for wood, small farmers had fled and the soil was depleted.

And then came the Civil War.

The Civil War

Before the Civil War, Vermont belonged to the young. In 1800, two-thirds of the population was under twenty-five years old. The settled population grew up and made families, enduring years of drought and flood, the War of

1812 and the eight-year embargo of trade with Canada. And then came the winter of 1816. Beginning in July, the temperatures dipped below freezing. Crops were ruined. Families fled—or died. Abby Hemenway's *Gazetteer* quotes Mrs. Gale: "It was all hardship." Newly opened stores closed and manufacturing sank to 20 percent of its turn-of-the-century level. Even when the first railroads were cut through in 1848, they did not bring economic salvation. Instead, they brought competition into Vermont, and began the decade-long run-up to the Civil War and its searing toll on the state's new generation.

The Civil War had a wrenching effect on the country, perhaps greatest in Vermont. The state had already abolished slavery in its republic's constitution of 1777. Before the Civil War, general stores became part of the Underground Railroad, smuggling freed slaves to Canada because, as noted by Barbara Radcliffe Rogers, "no one took any special notice when large boxes were loaded and unloaded there."

Abolitionist John Brown had a place in Vermont's heart, and his funeral cortège was met by mourners on every stop through the state in January of 1860, including in Panton, where the local surgeon's home on the crossroads would eventually become the Panton General Store. A year later, the Vermont Brigade was first organized from five infantry regiments, becoming part of the Union Army of the Potomac. Although it jubilantly sang "John Brown's Body" as it marched through Charles Town, West Virginia, where

Brown had been tried and hanged, it also suffered the highest number of casualties of any brigade in U.S. history, with the deaths of 1,172 volunteers. In all, Vermont sent 34,000 soldiers to war, losing more than a sixth of them. Along with Michigan and Kansas, Vermont saw the highest proportion of its citizens fighting in the Civil War. Vermont's 1860 population was 314,120—meaning about 10 percent of the population served, and 1 out of every 60 Vermonters died in that conflict.

After the war, those young veterans returned having now seen the world. They came home to families, eyes open, packing up and leaving Vermont for the West and the South and the promise of a new life away from the hardscrabble farms and blankets of unforgiving snow. Following on the heels of the Civil War was the Panic of 1873, when adoption of the gold standard bankrupted farmers and storekeepers with heavy silver-backed debt, driving Northeastern families into grinding poverty. Half of the veterans left the state, along with a generation of young people hoping to avoid Vermont's poor farms. Sons did not take over their fathers' stores, and many changed hands or closed in the third quarter of the nineteenth century. A staggering 40 percent of the young people abandoned Vermont villages and towns.

Not until the late 1880s were new general stores built in East Montpelier, Newfane, Danville, Norwich, Stowe and East Burke.

Late into the Twentieth Century

By the end of the nineteenth century, the nation was in the throes of a monetarism debate—and into the fray were brought the farmers of America. In his "Cross of Gold" speech, William Jennings Bryan said, "The great cities rest upon our broad and fertile prairies. Burn down your cities and leave our farms, and your cities will spring up again as if by magic; but destroy our farms and the grass will grow in the streets of every city in the country." Vermonters turned their backs on Bryan. Even after the sheep craze, farms had continued to grow to a peak of 35,522 in 1880, averaging about 140 acres each. Then they began to close, with Vermont losing 3,000 farms by the time of Bryan's 1892 speech.

The seeds were sown, however, for Vermont's future. In 1891, a publicity service was begun—the first in the nation, becoming the Bureau of Publicity in 1911. Automobiles arrived bursting with tourists; lakefront property was acquired; summer camps were founded, such as Roxbury's Teela-Wooket, where the train would stop and dozens of children debark. The young equestrians would take the five-minute walk to the town's country stores. In two decades the ski industry would get underway, enriching towns like Warren, whose general store would be transformed into a tourist mecca.

But before skiing came more troubles. After Vermonter Calvin Coolidge left the presidency to Herbert Hoover and his Great Depression, there were fewer than 25,000 farms left in the state. The number did not stop shrinking: 23,500 remained in 1940. The state's population grew a slim 7 percent over seventy-five years, with families abandoning their farms and moving away or relocating into Vermont's small cities.

The Great Depression itself was an anomaly in Vermont. The pain of downcountry cities did not reach into the rural north. Parents recounted to their children that the Depression may have pained the rest of the nation, but life in Vermont was so harsh that they never realized those pre-Depression years had been the *good* times. Only Vermont and Rhode Island had no bank closures during 1931. Life was almost normal, with the legendary frugality of the state's citizens giving rise to stories of Vermonters who carefully tucked away useless short bits of string in a box labeled "string too short to use."

During those tough days, farms increasingly needed the country stores for goods and credit. Jon St. Amour assembled the history of his Jericho Center store, learning that in the 1890s, the Jordan brothers wrote to their customers putting an end to credit. The subsequent owners extended credit, but letters withdrawing it went out again in the 1930s, and once more in the twenty-first century as belts tightened. Chief Lone Cloud of the Evansville Trading Post recalled "the favors local merchants have done for others over the years. They helped so many people extending credit, offering discounts and cashing checks when folks really needed it."

The 1930s also brought something else to Vermont: supermarkets. The Vermont Grocers' Association was formed in 1934 to represent supermarkets and general stores alike. From Bennington to Brattleboro, Orleans to Burlington, supermarkets pressured the general store.

State Representative Bill Keogh recalled the general store of his youth, a market on Burlington's Church Street—now a pedestrian mall—owned by Albert and Omer Verret. New competition arrived under the banners of Atlantic & Pacific, First National and Grand Union. Keogh says, "In the mid-1940s, customers went to their independent grocer's and ordered items. The grocer would go to the shelf to pick off the items and assembled them on the shelf in front of the customer. The customer would pay cash or the grocer would pull out the credit slip to add to the customer's total. Families would pay their bills on payday."

The Verrets, seeing the future, built a new supermarket on Shelburne Road. "That supermarket was the 'cat's meow' in those days," says Keogh. The innovation in supermarkets was picking one's own fresh fruits and vegetables, taking cans off the shelf and asking the meat cutter for the best cut of steak, putting everything into a basket to check out. Verret's delivered groceries and took back bottles with a two-cent deposit.

Electrification became a major issue in Vermont. Power was being extended across America, including the towns and villages. By the 1930s, it had become largely a rural question, affecting the smallest towns and their village stores. In his 1935 inaugural, Governor Charles Smith declared, "It seems probable that something may be accomplished in the near future regarding rural electrification. Vermont is backward in this respect. The period of the kerosene lamp is past. It is time that the farmer and his wife have the help of electricity at a price within their means." Governor George Aiken presided over the modernization through his farewell in 1941, and Governor Mortimer Proctor revealed in his 1945 inaugural that "68.8% of our 21,772 farms are now electrified and another 6.3% are so located as to be available for electrification."

Raymond Smith, far from the main roads in West Arlington, wrote about Smith's Cash Store, "In 1939 my father started running the store. At that time there was a gasoline-powered 32-volt DC generator in the cellar and a large shelf of wet-cell batteries. The generator was not in use at that time as the store had been rewired for commercial power. The 32-volt DC generator was quite old at that time and had probably been installed in the early 1920s."

Phone lines came through as well, reaching as far as Alburgh in 1904. Vermont had entered the modern era, from electrification to Great Depression to two great wars. Vermont's service in the Great War is not heralded, yet 14,000 citizens served and 642 died in Europe, resulting in tragedies in almost every town, including five from Dorset, three from Morrisville and one from Northfield.

World War II had the greatest impact on the state in the first half of the twentieth century. Approximately 50,000 soldiers from Vermont served—one-seventh of its entire population—and 1,233 did not return. Children took their parents' place in working the farms and store counters. Another 13,000 left the farms and villages to work in Springfield's machine tool industry. But Vermont's poverty—the poverty that had made the Great Depression seem normal—was evident, as half the military enlistees were rejected for physical ills, particularly malnutrition.

At war's end, thirty-three thousand soldiers came back, finding Vermont largely unchanged. Joe Sherman wrote,

> *There were those countless farms, the villages, the small mills. And little promise for the future. Thousands decided to leave Vermont. They wanted possibilities and newness, not the same old jobs and dirt roads and low standard of living most Vermonters had accepted—it seemed like forever—as their inheritance and destiny. By the hundreds, month after month, they packed their bags, hugged loved ones good-bye, wiped away the tears, and headed out into the mid-twentieth century.*

Companies moved south and eventually out of the country, and the last vast mills of New England—old, inefficient and expensive—shut down. There was no overflow for Vermont, and its own mills lost their markets. For those who stayed, the baby boom had begun. Vermont's change was underway.

And Verret's market-turned-supermarket was soon gone, replaced with a car dealership.

TRANSPORTATION,
INDUSTRY AND NATURE

Jerry's is
and is in
the center of the town.
It's not the place that used to be something else
and got converted to its present use. It's always been
a place for food and vehicles. First as a store and stable
and a wheelwright's shop, then, with cars, a store and gas pumps,
a mechanic and a lift. A place, since it began, to serve
two of the very few necessities: food and transportation.
–David Budbill, "Jerry's Garage," from Judevine

Vermont is outlined by the Connecticut River on the east and Lake Champlain on the west—both ideal transportation routes for a young, independent republic. From the 1790s through the 1820s, logs were strapped together into rafts complete with a crew house as they were floated south on Champlain to market. Ferries on the Connecticut from Fairlee to Orford, New Hampshire, carried people, horses, cattle, carriages and goods starting in 1774. By 1927, the eighty-four-cabin ferry *Franklin* was part of the intense competition on the lake.

But water did not become a Vermont trademark. Instead, Vermont's roads have been notorious for two hundred years.

Roads Make Way

Initially there were crossroads and short carriage routes from major towns downcountry. Goods and people could come to the new little Commonwealth of Vermont in the Green Mountains. Next came the American Revolution, with the Bayley-Hazen Military Road built away from British eyes along mountainsides and notches from Newbury on the Connecticut to Hazen's Notch near Canada.

And then came the turnpikes, beginning the slow connection of Vermont to itself and the rest of the country. The Vermont Legislature authorized the first turnpike ("a public highway from the south line of this state to the north line of the town of Newbury") to connect to the Bayley-Hazen Road in 1795. With that turnpike, the first public road to run the length of Vermont would be open.

Private companies were tempted by profit. The First Vermont Turnpike Corporation was chartered in

November 1796, with the power to take over land, lay out roads and build highways with gates. More turnpikes were authorized two years later under similar terms, including Rutland west to Salem in New York, Vergennes north to Burlington and extensions of the Connecticut Post Road.

These turnpikes were precursors of today's toll roads—only more expensive. One dollar at that time is worth about seventeen dollars today.

Coach, Phaëton, Chariot or other four-wheeled vehicle, drawn by two horses...$0.75
If drawn by four horses...................................$1.00
If drawn by more than four for each additional horse $0.06
Cart, Waggon, Sled or Sleigh drawn by two oxen or horses...$0.50
Each additional ox or horse...............................$0.06
Chaise, Chair or other Carriage drawn by one horse $0.37
Man and Horse..$0.25
Foot passenger $0.04
Horses, oxen, and other neat cattle, no in teams each $0.06
Sheep and swine, each.....................................$0.01

The doctor poses with his ox-drawn phaëton in front of the erstwhile store in Greensboro Bend. It is not known whether the doctor, the cart or the ox were new enough to draw a crowd. *Courtesy Greensboro Historical Society.*

More than two dozen private turnpikes were built in Vermont over the next fifty years, including the ambitious Green Mountain Turnpike, chartered in 1799, which ran from Clarendon to the Connecticut River at Bellows Falls—approximately the path later taken by the Rutland Railroad and by Vermont Route 103 today, through the towns of Rockingham, Shrewsbury, Mount Holly, Ludlow, Cavendish and Chester. The charter agreements allowed the turnpike owners to earn back expenses and generate income, and then return the road to the state.

The profit-encouraging charters also meant that turnpikes would follow the most economically lucrative course— existing trails, river valleys and mountain notches. Even so, Vermont is not an easy state to traverse. Some turnpikes were planked roads. The Lamoille County Plank Road was likely the first in New England, made of milled boards rather than logs dropped in place with gravel—the infamously uncomfortable "corduroy roads." Ward Knapp in his personal *History of Waterbury* recalls planked roads built of four-inch hemlock; other documented planked roads were built from Glastenbury to Searsburg and Vergennes to Bristol. There was an enthusiasm for planked roads, which were relatively easy to build and maintain in Vermont's harsh winters and muddy springs. Logs called stringers were first put on the road in the direction of travel, and then hemlock planks eight or more feet long and three to four inches thick were placed across the stringers. With drainage ditches along the roadside, planked roads offered a relatively smooth surface and speedy travel.

Not everyone was happy with turnpikes. In fact, creative locals built their own roads, such as Old Shunpike Road, which cuts through Shrewsbury and Mount Holly, deliberately bypassing the tollbooths on the Green Mountain Turnpike. Turnpikes affected trade, enabling a cash economy, keeping the local store local and encouraging itinerants to settle, while allowing farmers to travel unimpeded; tolls were not charged for farmers at work.

The main road through Greensboro was dirt, but like many sidewalks of the day, this one leading out of town was planked. *Courtesy Greensboro Historical Society.*

Local materials always found their way into roads. South Northfield was once called Slab City because its roads were built from locally quarried slate slabs—anything but mud! In contemporary times, where unpaved roads are still the rule away from major roads, local gravel along with remnants from quarries' slag heaps—crushed marble and granite dust—hold the surface stable.

The history of Vermont's roads explains the persistence of its village culture and the location of its country and general stores. The main road through Taftsville was the Windsor-Woodstock Turnpike, where the Taftsville Country Store has stood since the 1840s. It veered south toward what is present-day Vermont Route 12 about a half-mile east of the store. What is now U.S. Route 4 was built in the early 1850s as the "new road"—the southern boundary of the Taft Industrial Lot that was created and auctioned in 1855. When the store was built it fronted the turnpike, but now the current incarnation of that road dead-ends a quarter-mile west of the store in a cluster of mostly very old homes.

Near the Taftsville Country Store, the Quechee Gorge forced all roads to choose between sides of the Ottauquechee River. The main road to White River Junction before the gorge was on the far bank of the river, which is River Road from Woodstock through Quechee, then down the Quechee Road to the banks of the White River and into White River Junction. In the mid-nineteenth century, the gorge was spanned only by rail; autos could not cross until the railroad was closed in 1933 and the bridge was rebuilt.

Roads had become a tangled web, with 246 highway commissioners. The year 1898 brought the position of state highway commissioner, and projects were begun to fix the roads that were famous for their scenic beauty but often miserably maintained.

A heavy cask of molasses is rolled into the basement of F.H. Gillingham's in Woodstock. Six men hold it back as the team of horses (and neighborhood dog) stands by. Spare cartwheels are visible. *Courtesy Frank Billings, Woodstock.*

Once the roads were in some measure of repair and some were even paved as the twentieth century got underway, it was possible for Vermont to join lower New England. In 1922, the New England Road Marking System was developed, with yellow rectangular signs on posts and poles. The numbers will be familiar today: Route 9 from Bennington to Maine, Route 12A from Randolph to Northfield, Route 14 from White River Junction to Burlington and Route 25A from Topsham to Waits River. Visitors could find their way around Vermont without stopping to ask for landmarks.

What comes to visitors' minds first about Vermont's scenic roads are its covered bridges. There were six hundred covered bridges one hundred years ago, but the flood of 1927 carried four hundred of them away. Of the remaining, one hundred have survived fires and development into the present, with twenty under private ownership. The oldest extant covered bridge was built in 1808 in Middlebury, and the newest was built in Tunbridge in 2004 to replace one lost to an ice jam.

There are two explanations of why bridges were covered: to let horses cross without being spooked; or to protect the structure of the bridge from the elements. Considering that the popular Morgan is so even-tempered and that Vermonters are very frugal, the latter explanation is widely accepted. The shortest bridges are just 37 feet in Randolph and West Windsor; the longest, at 269 feet, is in Dummerston.

Four years later, the U.S. Highway System was inaugurated. U.S. Routes 2, 4, 5, 7 and 9 supplanted the New England System. Paving increased, but Vermont was still not an easy travel, especially in winter. Another change was coming: the

National Defense Highway System, quickly dubbed "the interstates," outlined the east border and slashed diagonally through the center of the state.

Interstate 91 opened in Brattleboro on November 1, 1958— Vermont's first divided highway—replacing U.S. Route 5 as the eastern route. By 1969, the entire system was finished, bringing travelers and exiles by the thousands. Vermont no longer appeared to be the forbidding landscape of its past. But the roads' effect on the country and general stores was profound. Along the Connecticut River, dozens of businesses were now bypassed. Vermont's first town of Windsor, which had fought to keep an interstate exit ramp from cascading into downtown, began to shrink, losing its country store as the plentiful tourist traffic now flashed by at freeway speeds. Through the center of Vermont, stores that had served locals and tourists—in Hartford, Sharon, South Royalton, Bethel, Randolph Center, Brookfield, Northfield, Barre, Waterbury, Jonesville and Richmond—were now almost entirely local, no more than names on an exit sign. The retail communities around Bolton contracted without an exit, whereas the lazy village and farming community a few miles north at Tafts Corners became a wilderness of big box stores. Even the U.S. Route 4 bypass, emulating an interstate, left Castleton Village behind. Rural areas shrank and interstate service towns grew. Suburbs appeared. More change was coming.

Now accessible to the rest of America, 1970 Vermont was in a different century than 1960 Vermont.

The Railroads

Not since the clearing of forests began in earnest was Vermont so transformed by human events. The railroads moved towns from hillside centers to valleys, brought manufactured goods and travelers to the state and made possible the growth of the great stone industry.

The first interstate railway service arrived in Vermont under the banner of the Vermont and Massachusetts Railroad, pulling into Vernon station in 1849. After six years of legislative permissions and roadbed and rail construction, the line ran from Brattleboro south all the way to Fitchburg, Massachusetts. Interstate railroads changed distant travel, of course, but also changed local travel. They knit together towns whose people could not travel through the mud and dirt. They crossed rivers and gorges for the first time, and for decades, as with the Quechee Gorge, rail was the only way to cross. Even the "traction railways"—streetcars—altered the path of commerce in such towns as Bellows Falls, Bennington or between Barre and Montpelier, where the seven-mile stretch could be traveled quickly. And with the ability to carry heavy freight in quantity, rail allowed the stone industry to ascend the economic ladder.

Building the railroads was an engineering achievement. The same lines found on the railroad maps from the 1870s are the ones being used today—despite the grades being calculated by hand with simple surveying tools. Fill was brought in, bridges were built, mountains were blasted away and the lines were run straight and true from one end of Vermont to the other. Classic roundhouses and turntables were found in every major town. Hundreds of stone arches, iron trusses and wooden "matchstick" bridges were constructed: stone in Brattleboro and Manchester, stone and iron in Hartland and Windsor, metal in Newport and Alburgh, metal and concrete in Newport and Duxbury and a wooden matchstick for the ill-fated Harlow Bridge in Northfield that went up in flames and was soon followed by a spectacular and deadly crash during its reconstruction.

Some of the most dramatic railroad building took place in the quarries near Barre. Building these railroads from the river valley up to the quarries demanded brilliant engineering, determined and patient investors and powerful locomotives.

The Quarries

Quarries appeared across Vermont beginning with the 1785 marble quarry in South Dorset. Stone was found everywhere in the glacier-carved hills: marble, granite, slate, talc, copper, serpentine asbestos, verde antique. One hundred Vermont towns joined the quarry list, from Athens and Andover to Roxbury and Washington. Even copper mining was tried and failed.

The "Granite Capital of the World" began when Thomas Courser and Robert Parker opened the first granite quarry in the United States just south of Barre in 1814; another opened on the opposite hillside in 1825. More opened until there was a vast sprawl of quarries south of town. Granite was transported in winter, when farmers' animals were not occupied in the fields, with teams of twenty-four horses or a dozen oxen dragging sleds of granite down the steep slopes into Barre. The process was slow and dangerous.

The railroads might have changed this scene earlier, except that industrialist and former Governor Charles Paine wanted his new Vermont Central Railroad to travel through his hometown of Northfield instead of via the more accommodating Williamstown Gulf. The railroad, completed in 1843, bypassed Barre on its run from the Massachusetts border to St. Albans, taking on the rise to the highest point on the through-line from Miami to Montréal over tiny Roxbury, where three country stores and, before it burned, a grand hotel served travelers to Vermont.

Although a railroad to Barre and Montpelier was finally built in 1873—during the economic panic that swept the United States—it did not solve the problem of the transport of granite, which still made the descent into Barre via animal for six quarry companies with 50 stonecutters employed. Finally, in December 1888 the first load of granite throttled down the hill via the Sky Route to great celebration— and four years later, more than one hundred companies employed some 1,500 workers. Over 500,000 tons of granite were carried on 30,000 cars during the first eight years of the Barre Railroad.

Downtown Barre became a maze of tracks, crossings, competing rail companies and acres of granite sheds. Thousands of employees had cash to spare, and needed to spend it. So came about the nomadic Dente's Market. Basilio Dente and James Catterello were among the hundreds of Italian immigrants who settled in Barre along with granite sculptors and tradespeople. They opened the Boston Fruit Store in 1907 to serve the families of many of their countrymen in the granite industry with fresh carrots, potatoes, watermelons, plums and even pineapples and bananas. The store flourished, Basilio bought out his partner in a few months and the market soon outgrew the tiny brick building (today occupied by a shop called Coins & Hobbies). In 1915, the market moved to larger quarters across Main Street, where it continued to prosper. Basilio and his wife Mary bought the entire block of stores, moving their business a few doors down, all while the "Granite Capital of the World" continued to grow up around Dente's. Soon their son James took over and ran the business for twenty-seven years; Basilio died in 1956, after nearly a half-century behind the counter.

In 1972, the aggressive interstate highway growth claimed several properties. The "Beltway" split from the main access road to I-89 into downtown, forcing Dente's Market to move once more, just a few doors away. James's son Rick took over the market in its new location until more comfortable quarters became available—and within months Dente's had moved yet again to a Main Street location, where it has served its clientele for the past thirty-five years. In a century, Dente's could be found in five locations hardly two hundred yards apart.

Rail affected towns throughout the state. Rural towns such as Marshfield had service, as the Montpelier & Wells River Railroad arrived in 1873. By 1880, fully 10 percent of Proctor's population—more than 1,500 workers, almost the population of all of Proctor today—worked in its marble industry.

Railroads then began a decline. The 1862 flood damaged many rail lines, but it was the flood of November 1927 that truly wreaked havoc on the railroads, downing bridges and undermining track; heavy locomotives and even full trains toppled into the water and mud. The Great Depression took away stone markets, and many quarries closed. Buyers wanted smaller lots and took to using trucks on Vermont's improved main roads.

Though military traffic was high during World War II, by the late 1940s passenger rail was all but dead, and freight was struggling with change. With diesel technology in 1949, Newport had a "graveyard" of steam engines headed north to Montréal for scrapping. Mail that had been handled by trains into the 1950s began to be carried by trucks and

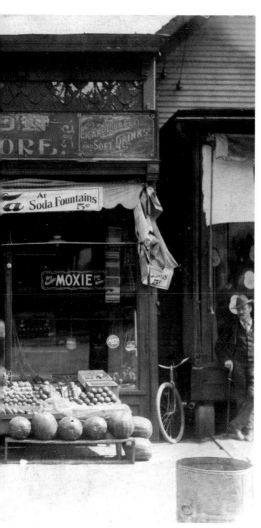

Basilio and Mary Dente exhibit the wide array of fresh fruit that arrived by train for their Boston Fruit Store, founded in 1907. *Courtesy Rick Dente, Barre.*

Basilio Dente poses in his newly expanded market in 1915, moved across the street from his original Boston Fruit Store in Barre. *Courtesy Rick Dente, Barre.*

airplanes. Stations closed. The interstate highway arrived in Vermont in the late 1950s and was done by 1969. Although the first hangar at Burlington Airport had been built in 1929, it was the 1970s that saw its expansion into a busy terminal.

April 30, 1958, saw the final run down the Sky Route into Barre.

The Age of Tourism

Tourists made some country stores profitable for the first time—Dorset, Warren and Woodstock among them—as they began coming to Vermont to ski, fish, hunt, hike, camp, bike, boat, ride, snowmobile and "leafpeep."

Yes, Baron von Trapp brought his singing family to the hills up the road from Shaw's dry goods store in Stowe, but they were not the first to "ski Vermont." The state had no skiing tradition; winter travel had been by snowshoe since the military forces of the independent Commonwealth of Vermont in 1783.

Skiing first appeared as a sport after the Civilian Conservation Corps cut ski trails into the Green Mountains in 1933. F.H. Gillingham's store in Woodstock sold skis in 1934 when a nearby ski tow opened. Ski racing started on Mount Mansfield in 1934, with the first chairlift in 1938 and the first derby in 1946. The CCC's little cabins grew into ski areas, and by the 1950s hundreds of visitors were making the ten-hour trek from Connecticut along Vermont's narrow, winding U.S. highways.

The interstates cut travel time in half, and by the mid-1960s, the ski areas were bustling on winter weekends. But the interstates also began segregating newcomers from old-timers. According to Joe Sherman, the skiers gathered at new bars and avoided the country stores and their local clientele.

On the other hand, the country store did provide a link for transitory activities such as hunting, fishing, hiking and snowmobiling. Hiking to Mount Mansfield was once done in Victorian skirts, but the trail cut by the CCC and later maintained by the Green Mountain Club allowed hikers to make pilgrimages up and down the Long Trail. With seventy shelters along the way, the trail was ideal for individuals yearning for a month's solitude. Stevie Balch, an "end-to-ender" who solo-hiked the Long Trail's 270-mile length from Canada to Massachusetts in 1970, recalled stopping at the Jonesville Store for supplies and, later, hungry for food not heated fairly past lukewarm over the campfire, she took a break from the wilderness by hiking down the mountain to West Wardsville—for pizza.

Likewise, the country stores offer warmth and friendship for snowmobilers. The Vermont Association of Snow Travelers was organized in 1967, its volunteers from 135 clubs building the first unified snow trail marking system in the United States—80 percent of it running across private property. VAST trails are carefully designed to pass by the stores with their warm wood stoves and pots of coffee, whether the ridgeline Floyd's in Randolph Center or the lakeside Hastings in West Danville.

Country stores also provide fishing supplies. Lakes like Bomoseen, St. Catherine, Groton, Elmore, Fairlee, Dunmore, Hortonia, Rescue, the great Champlain, the border-crossing Memphremagog and lake-sized reservoirs offer fishing that

Silver Lake was as prime a recreation spot in the 1930s as it is today. Here the Barnard General Store (left) is crowded with merrymakers. *Courtesy Barnard Store*.

begins in early spring and goes through the summer season. Even before stocking, fish were plentiful. In 1918, eleven tons of fish—about twenty thousand fish—were caught on Bomoseen and St. Catherine. Barnard's quiet Silver Lake was long a favorite for fishing, boating and swimming, and the Barnard General Store was the gathering place for hundreds of holidays, weddings and celebrations.

Hunting was not so much a sport as a way of survival in Vermont. Deer camp was the culture's "coming of age" event for young people, a first night of darkness and fire and a frosty morning of learning to be still and focused and become part of the hunt. Deer camp continues as autumn's deeply significant event, and while hunting is now more sport than survival, the deer are never wasted, becoming part of the cold winter's diet. Hunting season draws visitors, with country stores providing licenses for hunting deer, turkey, bear, wildfowl and fish; selling guns and ammunition, bows and arrows, lines and lures, worms and clothing; and acting as official game reporting stations—and posting the results for local "buck pools."

Arts and culture are not latter-day developments in Vermont. With their high literacy rate, Vermonters prided themselves in schoolhouses and opera houses, with grand buildings in the geographically distant towns of Derby Line, Vergennes, Randolph, Bennington, Barre, Enosburg Falls and Bellows Falls. The Vermont Symphony Orchestra, founded in 1934, is the only remaining state symphony in the nation. Chamber music festivals from Marlboro and Killington, symphonic "Made in Vermont" ten-town tours and weeklong reggae, jazz and country music events all sell their tickets at local country stores.

New to Vermont is agri-tourism. Beginning with fall foliage rides a half-century ago and encouraged by the no-billboards rule, "leafpeeping" is today combined with visits to working farms, cider mills, sugarhouses, cheese producers, wood mills and equestrian venues. The aggressive marketing of the Vermont brand, from *Vermont Life* magazine to the Agriculture Department's Seal of Quality, has shifted the state's image from the poor backwoods to the northland's Garden of Eden.

THE UNTOLD STORY
PHILOSOPHY, STRUGGLE
AND REDEMPTION

Vermonters never loved their country stores, never recount store stories. Churches and meetinghouses and inns and houses are local characters, but save for David Budbill's *Judevine*, Walter Hard's *A Mountain Township* or Nancy Tschorn's *Country Store Stories*, the lowly store escapes memory.

Abby Hemenway's massive *Vermont Gazetteer* runs some 1,400 pages. In the 74 pages dedicated to the history of Stowe, we learn about the election of the first fence viewer (a post still extant in some Vermont towns) and the sealer of leather (who approved the quality of leather to assure no one was injured or killed while riding), we are given the construction and sizes of the schoolhouse and "a good sized public house" and several complete sermons—but only passing mention is made of those who founded the town's first stores.

There were blacksmiths in Rutland in 1779 and Shrewsbury in 1785, but when Timothy Dwight toured Vermont in 1803, his talk about farms and sawmills made no mention of shops or general stores. The oldest general store in Hartland would not be started until 1805. Wrote Jan Albers in *Hands on the Land*, "The structures of the community—taverns, schools, churches, lawyers' offices, and general stores—were beginning to appear, usually in about that order." Even Beach Conger in *Bag Balm and Duct Tape* sees the country store as a village center's last appendage: "On the common itself are the town hall, the Grange, the Congregational church, and, if it has sufficient lineage, a general store."

When stores did arrive, barter often ruled transactions as much as cash. The general store in West Dover never closed and kept detailed records, accepting barter as often as hard currency. In Woodstock, an 1832 barter book turned up during renovation, where an ounce of cloves or a yard of ribbon was valued at six cents.

Perhaps it was the European bias against merchants that persisted in the new world. Perhaps it is merely that we do not appreciate what is familiar. And perhaps that is why country store owners so often look unhappy in their photos and are legendarily grouchy.

Those who do remember were usually the ones running a store. Corinne Wilder Thompson ran the Jericho Center store for many years, recalling her own childhood. "I was six or seven. I remember coming in and getting penny candy. They had Kits, oh, and Bazooka gum—that was everyone's favorite. Mr. Nealy sold everything. It was like Wal-Mart. He had clothes, tools, hardware, groceries. Everything."

An 1832 barter book turned up during construction at F.H. Gillingham's in Woodstock. Ten yards of silk were valued at $5.40, a gallon of molasses at $0.50 and eight pounds of butter at $1.00. *Courtesy Frank Billings, Woodstock.*

Everything. Like a Wal-Mart…but more responsive to local needs. If you couldn't sell it, you didn't stock it—or, as the sign says, "If we don't have it, you don't need it." Thomas Naylor and William Willimon explained in *Downsizing the U.S.A.*, "The traditional Vermont general store was a precursor to the shopping mall. In the not too distant past, it was not uncommon for a general store to include a grocery store, an apothecary, a post office, a pub, a barbershop, and a doctor's office."

Indeed, by the turn of the twentieth century, country stores sold everything—including opium and kits of chair repair parts. Yes, the opium made in Northfield was from local poppies.

Give or take, there are today some three hundred country and general stores in Vermont. A handful are touristic outlets in historic buildings with nary a feed sack in sight; some are convenience stores whose country store roots have vanished; those in Mendon and Taftsville are the bricks-and-mortar sites where mail-order and Internet sales make up their true mass; others are true general stores serving a local population with groceries and dry goods, and a few such have even been resurrected from abandonment, such as the store in Woodbury; others have re-evolved as simpler stores, like J.J. Hapgood's in Peru, which is largely a pizza shop; some ballooned into mega-corporations like the Vermont Country Store itself; and then there are the dozen stalwart stores whose diverse inventories, personal customer knowledge and rambling structures identify an American institution that has survived from past to present—Dan & Whit's in Norwich, Evansville Trading Post, H.N. Williams in Dorset, Currier's in Glover and Hastings in West Danville.

The byword of the country store is change, not history or museumhood. So what *is* a real country store? In visiting stores for this book, the author was cross-examined by Ross Warren at the register in H.N. Williams Store. What qualifies as a country store, he wanted to know. How long did it have to be around? Was it a family store? Did it have everything—food, feed, clothes, hunting supplies, syrup? Was it for tourists or the local community? These are the questions faced by every country and general store owner, and they come down to a single almost existential quest: Why am I here?

But philosophy doesn't pay the bills—or combat disaster.

Fire

Rather than historical events, it was fire that determined the history of many of Vermont's country stores. Fire was merciless to home and business, and the wood-framed stores and even the brick ones with their wood floors and flammable merchandise were devastated. News accounts are found in every paper, every year. Stores perished. The Lunenburg Store in 1866; an entire block of stores in Brattleboro in 1869 and a block in Randolph in 1877; Porter's Store in

Springfield in 1882; the McCain & Manahan Store in South Royalton in 1883, and all of downtown Randolph in 1884; an entire block of Burlington's downtown stores in 1887; the Bridgewater Corners store arson in 1889; both Castleton and Newfane stores in 1890; Lougee Bros. & Smythe's in the great St. Johnsbury fire of 1892; Ira E. Hunt's General Store in Fairfax in 1898; the century ending with the fiery loss of the Paine block in Northfield in 1899.

These disasters continued into the modern era, with Merchant's Row in Rutland burning in 1903; the entirety of Hyde Park lost in 1910; every town in Orleans County except Morgan having a fire in 1911; the downtown square of Bellows Falls with ten businesses and the Windham Hotel burning in 1912; the Grange block of Brattleboro and the Union block of Montpelier destroyed in 1914; and Montpelier's Lawrence block gone in 1924. W.H. Greene's store in Franklin and the Hotel Coolidge in White River Junction both were lost to fire in 1925, Baxter's Store in Marlboro was devastated in 1931 and a quarter-century later it didn't end, with Hebblethwaite's Store in Peacham burned in 1959. Even the emphasis on fire protection and quick response in recent times could not save the sweep of fire through an entire block of stores in downtown Randolph in 1991 and central St. Johnsbury in 2000. The historic Country Store in Montpelier, on its site since 1850, was wiped out in the fire in the spring of 2003, and another block of stores in Enosburg was razed by flames in 2005.

A.H. Bailey's was untouched, but J.A.R. Corwin & Sons burned to the ground in the great fire of 1926 in Chelsea. *Courtesy Will Gilman, Chelsea.*

Fire was the great leveler, even if one general store like A.H. Bailey's in Chelsea was spared by the 1926 fire that swept through downtown and stopped next door, destroying the J.A.R. Corwin general store.

And much of what was not destroyed by fire was lost to the great flood of 1927. Vermont became a symbol of loss. Farms became fields with only stone walls, lilacs and day lilies to remind visitors of their existence.

Technology also dealt a death blow to the country stores. News gathered at the country store could now be spread by telephones. In towns like East Burke—which once had a store for harnesses, feed, supplies and buckets, another for mops, food, dry goods and cloth and a third for hardware, machinery and coffins—there was left only one. F.H. Dean's old store in Monkton, long and narrow, kept raw materials on the second floor, so hogsheads, barrels of molasses or sacks of flour and sugar were brought up by block and tackle. No more. In the mid-twentieth century, the elms disappeared from main streets across Vermont and America, symbols of the loss of the stolid general store in calm and crisis.

In the background have been three challenges. The first was the supermarkets of the 1930s, which gave customers the ability to pick their own products. The second challenge was the appearance of convenience stores, where a limited selection of goods was combined with fuel and opportunistic placement for modern-day travel. In New Haven, Bert Sargent explained that the old general store became a Jiffy Mart, even while it stayed in the original building. Today, that building is being replaced. With the suburban sprawl from Burlington eastward, vast tracts of land were prime locations for convenience stores, fast-food outlets—and the third challenge.

Because of Vermont's strong environmental laws, big box stores arrived late. It was the last state to allow a Wal-Mart, but in they came, followed by big boxes in every large town. Charles Morrissey wrote, "Vermont parents buy more at chain stores in shopping centers than at general stores or the little mom-and-pop stores which manage to survive."

Village Culture

Stores are critically important to a village culture, and
Vermont is a village culture.
—Jay Hathaway

Vermonters are proud and isolationist. Only one in five hundred Americans lives here. Once living in their own country, many want to secede again. Republican Senator Jim Jeffords became an independent before retiring. Conservatism may still be strong, but it finds the socialism of Senator Bernie Sanders accommodating to its populism. Its town meetings are democratic and vocal and it closely supervises elected officials and representatives. With a mere 608,000 people, Vermont has the highest proportion of elected officials of any state.

Despite Vermont towns being isolated—the road from Waterbury to Stowe was no more than a cow path until the early twentieth century—it did not keep people at home. Northfield's Wally Aseltine related how he used to go to dances in West Danville at the erstwhile dance hall across from the Hastings Store. The late Preston "Babe" Flint of Roxbury had photos of the local quarry's baseball team, and he traveled with his team to towns throughout the county.

These recollections *signify*. Vermont has a strong sense of place. Until the recent development of 911 emergency services, there were few street addresses. Ward Knapp recalled that locations were named for their last owners—Richardson's place or the White farm, or even a cellar hole that *used* to be Martin's place. So it is with stores—Buxton's in Orwell, Floyd's in East Randolph, Currier's in Glover. People and their places.

It's not all pretty, geographically or socially. There is the cluttered Barre-Montpelier Road, and poor towns like Snowsville and its packed general store. Eugenics surveys of the early twentieth century ominously hoped to perpetuate the "Vermont stock." In *Rural Vermont*, two hundred Vermonters contributed studies to the 1931 book. "The center of interest from the beginning was in the people," it read. "The health, the education, the religion, and the recreation of rural people were to be studied from the standpoint of their influence upon the quality of the life in the farm and village homes, their outlook and their ideals."

So what does it mean to remain true to an ideal—a country store ideal? Is there one? Is there *ever* an ideal in the business world? The country store occupies a unique place in both business and history—close to its customers in a state of ongoing mutation. Three unique viewpoints sum this up.

The Keys

Jon St. Amour, owner of the Jericho Center store, recalled Gerry and Lil Desso, owners of the store for more than thirty years. "They are still revered in this town; they did anything for anyone. They kept keys for the church, the community center, the library, and myriad houses. People still tell us from time to time, 'Lil would do this so why can't you' or something to that effect. I seek them out for advice; it amazes me that they could run this store for thirty years. I asked them once if they missed it. Lil smiled and shook her head no. 'I do miss the people, though.'"

Amour continued,

> In our first year here, my brother Mark had a room upstairs that you could get to by way of some back stairs. One night at ten o'clock, he was asleep and someone came banging on his back door. A woman had locked herself out of her house and she knew that she had left a spare key here some years ago. Unable to rouse my brother Mark from his sleep, she opened the unlocked back door and made her way into Mark's foyer. Mark finally awoke to see a woman pounding furiously on his door. Mark led her down into the store where she dug out her house key from a big brown bag full of spare keys. It was our first real introduction to what a country store means to a community.

Another sense of Vermont was reprinted nearly eighty years ago in *Rural Vermont*.

In a photo that looks like it could have been taken in 1906, these men warm themselves after a hard day at Machs' General Store in 2006. *Courtesy Marilyn Bellemare, Pawlet.*

The Homemaker's Creed

We believe that the family life of the Vermont home has in it all the elements needed for the successful building of character and citizenship.

That there abiding is a sense of permanence and security which makes for stability of character; a feeling of strength; an appreciation of the dignity and rhythm of labor; an awareness of the beauty of our surrounding hills; and high ideals of truth, justice and faith.

That through daily contact in the home with living and growing things comes a spiritual sense of nearness to the Giver of life.

That therein are developed a true hospitality, a kind neighborliness, an appreciation of the value of education, and a fine spirit of community cooperation.

We believe that for the enrichment of life, every home will provide its members with comforts and conveniences; maintain a high standard of health; afford opportunity through reading, recreation, and self-expression for the development of personal tastes.

We believe that groups of homes of this type will form an ideal community providing inspiring surroundings and stimulating contacts.

Thus will the finest traditions of Vermont be preserved.

There was no better observer of Vermont than Walter Hard, rock-ribbed Republican and mountain poet. Like David Budbill, he was one of the very few to remark on the country stores in his 1933 book *A Mountain Township.*

The Storekeeper

That small house with the dormer windows
Belongs to Eben Sedgwick, the storekeeper.
Eben really lives in his store on the corner.
You'll find him sitting on a stool

Posting his books on the high desk.
When the sun comes in through the window
It shimmers on the gauze of cobwebs.

Eben is short and he's getting heavy.
His hair is thin and white
But his beard is quite dark.
When he comes to wait on a customer
He always has a smile around his eyes.
Perhaps May Simpson, the dressmaker, wants buttons.
Eben will turn to a disorderly array of boxes.
He'll look over his glasses and sing: "Buttons, buttons."
Probably before May goes out Eben will suggest
Some lone man who needs a button sewer.

On the other side there are groceries.
Barrels of beans, corn meal, sugar—brown or white;
And of course one of fat Boston crackers.
Two cheeses, one mild and one strong,
Stand on the counter by the scales.
There's a barrel of kerosene by a cask of molasses.
A strange smell comes from the sawdust on the floor.

Then there's a counter with some store clothes on it.
In a wall case there is a shelf of lamps
And a pile of black hats such as Eben always wears.

Eben has never made more than a living.
Probably he isn't much of a merchant.
He is much more than a merchant.
Of course he's sung in the choir
And been school committeeman for years.
He's always on some board or the head of some committee.
But many of the things he does are only known to a few.

When he dies his executor will say harsh things
About many of the accounts on his books.
Eben knew he'd never get his pay
But he just had to help out
When there was so much trouble in the family.
But the things that never appear on books!
What a ledgerful Eben would have had!
Little kindnesses, a cheering word,
Advice, sugar-coated with a story.
Just a smile.

When Eben passes on
Some may wonder at the few dollars in the bank.
None will be surprised
At the number of his friends.

Country Store Philosophy
A job is what you do, not who you are—unless you own
and operate a country store.
—Nancy Tschorn

Stores may have been favorite places in town, but storekeepers were not always favorites.

In *Bag Balm and Duct Tape*, Beach Conger wrote about the fictional village of Dunster and the wonderfully Dickensian-named store owner Daniel Contremond ("God judge me, I'm against the world!"), who "was one of those uncommon people who folks like to believe is not: an honest man. Dan Contremond was also stubborn. He hung on to a business that lost money every year because he wouldn't change it, and for which, like a ton of cast-iron cookware he had in stock, there was no longer any market—except perhaps from tourists who were looking for a touch of Old Vermont to put in their new kitchen. But tourists didn't shop in Dunster."

Taftsville's Charlie Wilson has an uptake of the Vermont life that extends to storytelling. It seems that the proprietor of a country store ordered a keg of molasses shipped by train from a broker in New York. When the proprietor went to the train station to pick up his molasses, he found an invoice and a keg—but the molasses had leaked out during the trip. The proprietor, a frugal Vermonter, found use for both the wooden keg and the invoice in his wood stove. Months later, after repeated requests for payment went unanswered, the New York broker took action. He wrote to the stationmaster in Vermont to verify that the keg of molasses had arrived. He wrote to the president of the local bank, inquiring into the store owner's credit standing. He wrote to the mayor, asking for the name of a good lawyer to pursue the matter in court. Two weeks later the broker received a letter from Vermont. It said: "As the Stationmaster, I can inform you that your keg arrived; no molasses. As the President of the Bank, I can assure you that my credit is excellent. As the Mayor, I can tell you that I am the only lawyer practicing in these parts. And if I wasn't the Pastor of the church, I'd tell you to go to hell."

Wilson was not far from the truth. When Baxter's Store burned in September 1931, townspeople were unmoved; Merton Baxter was not a well-loved figure in Marlboro. The story is told that a little girl on her way home with a bag of sugar spilled it onto the muddy road. She ran back to the store in tears, and Baxter gave her a new bag—just the bag—with orders to pick up the sugar.

Baxter would never sell the last item of any article in his stock because he never wanted anyone to say he was out of anything. According to a letter from a woman who was a child when Baxter's Store was the only one in town, she remembers him as frightening and the store as dark and gloomy, with grim men sitting around a wood stove. She was not allowed to linger.

Merton Baxter's store on fire in Marlboro in 1931. The locals were delighted to see the smoke rising in the shape of a cross above the disliked storekeeper's building. *Reverend H. Shaw; courtesy Donald Sherefkin, Marlboro Historical Society.*

Baxter was also known to sell water to the local fire department before they could fight a blaze. So when Baxter's Store burned, some claimed to see a cross rising from the burning structure.

Stories about Baxter's grim presence were hardly rumor. Here is his correspondence with his supplier:

Marlboro, Vt. June 19th, 1930
Mr. C.M. Benson
       Brattleboro, Vt.

Dear Sir:-What Be I agoin to do with
These Few Loaves of Rye Bread as they call
it. I Orderd Wheat Bread as I Suposed.
Frank Chase wont Touch None of that Bread,
Mozart Lucier Want, Justin Thomas want Home
This Morning with No Bread. Mrs. Warnock
I had Trouble with her Last Night I dont
know as they will Trade any More with Me.
I Told them all that the Bread was Good
Enough, But they did not think so.
               Very Truly yours.
               M.E. Baxter

Marlboro, Vt., June 21st, 1930
Mr. C.M. Benson
       Brattleboro, Vt.

Dear Sir:- I should like 10 Fresh Loaves
of Wheat Bread. If you have it. And I had
Trouble with Earnest Brown on that Rye Bread
Business. I got so Mad I Throwed his Bread
all in to the Floor as Tight as I could
Jumper. So dont Never Send up no More Rye

Bread Here. Our People No Better then to
Want it. They will find Fault Pretty Quick
If Every Thing Aint just SO.
           Very Truly Yours.
           M.E. Baxter

After the fire, Merton Baxter went to live with his niece in Wilmington, Vermont. He never married.

Until recent times, storekeepers like these at the long-shuttered Windsor Store were not known for their sense of humor, but were always open to serve community needs—for a profit, of course. *Courtesy Charles Wilson, Taftsville.*

Storekeepers were often ground down by work, poor finances and unpaid customer credit. As they grew older, their stores grew as shopworn as they themselves. When Andy Mégroz bought the Panton Store, he says it "was not what you call classy. You could grow vegetables on the floor." The previous owner took little care, and the store had deteriorated from the handsome mid-nineteenth-century surgeon's home to a grubby shack of grimy shelves and unswept floors.

Sometimes the storekeepers were at wit's end. Charlie Wilson at Taftsville had yet another story about the store's previous owner. A New York woman (she could be from anywhere, but Charlie, the Los Angeles refugee, saw most of the Northeast outside of Vermont as "New York") came bursting into the store—busy, trying to make phone calls, kicking up a fuss about the store's poor choices and wanting some good cheese. No, not that one. Not that one. Not this one either. Yes—*that* one. But she was on a diet and didn't dare eat much, asking for the *very smallest* piece of cheese she could have. The owner, without missing a beat, offered, "I can let you smell the knife."

Corinne Wilder Thompson thought the storekeeper in Jericho Center not so much grouchy as strict. "You had to behave in there. He was very old fashion," she says.

On the other hand, the country store owner, especially today, has a renewed sense of customer service to add to the store's place in the community. The Waits River Store encourages good school grades with pizza specials; the

Eugene Booska is the storekeeper at Snowsville General in Braintree, where he presides over a hunter's paradise, from camp food to ammunition.

Wayside Store had a book-trading library and its owners know and greet every customer; in Newbury, the store sponsors yearly festival days. Where post offices once moved away, stores now fight to keep them.

When writer, shepherd and songwriter Linda Faillace was engaged in a bitter fight with the U.S. Department of Agriculture over her sheep during the mad cow scare, her tiny East Warren Schoolhouse Market became the focal point for community gatherings, protests and national media. The fight and the natural foods she sold in her store also brought attention to the country's growing organic foods movement, which has had strong roots in Vermont since the second wave of downcountry immigrants began arriving in the 1960s.

Architecture

Building country stores was a practical matter. There is no typical country store, even if the image is of a clapboarded building with four-posted porch and wagons straining with barrels and boxes. The country and general stores in Vermont were sometimes built as stores, but often were converted from homes or other shops. The Panton Store was a surgeon's house from 1848, and H.N. Williams in Dorset was a harness shop from 1840.

Of Vermont's motley stores, architectural historian Gary Lord writes,

> *Some are high style, but others are no longer of architectural interest because they have been radically altered over time and shorn of their historic fabric. They have been made over so many times it is difficult to discover anything original. Façades have been radically altered. Otherwise interesting antique buildings fall into the hands of thoughtless renovators who denigrate or destroy their character. Other buildings never had any architectural interest; they were built as utilitarian structures with no regard to style.*

An example of radical alterations is seen at the Chester Store. Built in 1849 as a simple building on the old Green Mountain Turnpike where the new Rutland Railroad was being laid, the store was almost solitary in the windswept, denuded plains of Windsor County. As trade expanded along the railroad in a town known for its Stone Village built from blocks of locally quarried gneiss, the front façade was added in about 1890 ("mercilessly if not hideously transformed," according to Lord).

The scene in Chester shows a lonely Leland's Store poised beyond the windswept field of snow beside the tracks of the Rutland Railroad. *Courtesy Lisai's Market, Chester.*

Fred A. Leland's original store in the late nineteenth century was a simple cottage, with attached horse stable in the back. *Courtesy Lisai's Market, Chester.*

The business was expanding, so a new façade was added to Fred A. Leland's Store in Chester in the early twentieth century. *Courtesy Lisai's Market, Chester.*

Lisai's Market in Chester as it looks today, with the added façade incorporated into the structure, along with a roof raised to a full story.

Trade trumped tradition in growing Vermont, and in the twentieth century, the store was once again expanded by lifting its half-story upper floor and creating full-sized living quarters for the owners. There was no National Register to preserve nearly tumbledown buildings for a touristic image of a quaint green state—and for most of the region's general stores, the byword is not preservation, but profit.

Today some stores have become images of their past as well as the present, such as the Original General Store in Pittsfield, with a European wine cellar in its former dank basement and carefully arrayed jars of candy and local products. Yet stores are in business—but not the museum business.

To the visitor, country stores seem to exist in beautiful places because a combination of factors have kept them alive, one of which is trade. A store without trade collapses in on itself, literally and figuratively. When H.N. Williams changed from harness shop to general store, it was during the aftermath of the Great Depression. And downtown, the village's tiny market—Peltier's, now the Dorset Union Store—saw its focus shift to the increasingly upscale clientele that was moving in from downcountry. In the poorer towns, even the traveling public could not save the stores. In Bethel, a mill town north of wealthy Woodstock and recreational Barnard with its Silver Lake, Richardson's Store closed in the late twentieth century when the family's younger generation was no longer interested in long hours and paltry rewards. After several tries and changes of ownership, the Moscow Store, just up the hill from ski-crazy Stowe and the famous Trapp Family Lodge, was shuttered in 2007. The Marshfield Store closed as this book was being finished.

Some changed hands and direction, such as the Danville General Store. Others closed and reopened with community help coupled with preservation funds—Woodbury is one of those. New owners changed the store approach in Taftsville with its strong Internet presence, and Northfield Falls reversed several years of historic focus for a convenience store approach. Even more dramatic is New Haven, where the old store has become a Jiffy Mart convenience store.

There's no love lost for the country store, even today. Indeed, the typical history of any general store is summed up in *Green Mountain Heritage*:

> *Ariel Edgerton is said to have built the first store at the Center. He was born in 1789 and came to Northfield in 1811. In 1815 he built a house and store, the first building erected for business purposes in Center Village, and which he continued to operate until 1819. This building burned about 1890 and was replaced by another building used as a store for many years which was finally taken down in 1966.*

Come, gone and not missed.

Thirty years ago, Charles Morrissey wondered what passing tourists might think about Vermont's little towns. Do they wonder who lives in trailers and tumbledown houses? He asked, "Do they notice the sad and ugly towns they drive through to get to the pristine villages which outsiders have restored?" He contrasted sooty Bellows Falls with "charming" Grafton, Bridgewater's forsaken mill town houses with nearby upscale Woodstock and "decrepit Hardwick, a false-fronted town which looks transplanted from the mined-out silver lodes of the West, [that] differs remarkably from Greensboro and Craftsbury Common, trim towns northward which gleam with bridal whiteness."

The country stores serve the populations of each of these towns differently, and some struggle to serve every population. External forces intervene, such as when tiny Middlesex was isolated by the flood of 1927 and nearby bridges had to be rebuilt quickly. Today Middlesex sits at the interstate gateway to the ski areas in Warren, Waitsfield and Fayston, where its store once served visitors on the Central Vermont Railroad and travelers on U.S. Route 2, long before the days of skiing in Vermont. Yet as times changed and the railroad ended its passenger service to the town—the station building exists, but is falling down—the modest 1840s-era Middlesex Country Store was hardly noticed by tourists because the road turned north over the bridge just a few hundred feet away, with the skiers roaring off the new interstate. The majority of the business was local, until the new iron bridge grew seventy years old and began to fail. The state surveyed the area and built a new bridge to Route 100B a few hundred feet north—turning at the Middlesex Country Store. According to owner Bob Fusco, the new bridge brought an uptick in trade and new life to his store.

Other stores simply *are*. In Adamant, the co-op store was a one-and-a-half-story residential cottage on a small three-corner crossroads, converted to commercial use. Save for the dress of the women and a few coats of paint, Adamant Co-Op looks unchanged in a century. Even the crossroads is still dirt.

Jay Hathaway called country stores tight, crowded and rickety, with "creaking floor, ringing bell, musty smell.

The Adamant Co-Op as a cottage in 1908. The women of the house stand on the porch. Another home is to the left and a barn behind, and the crossroads is dirt. *Courtesy Lois Toby, Adamant.*

The Adamant Co-Op as a store in 2008. The roads are identical—and still dirt—but the other home is gone and there is a new barn behind the store. The front door is now a window. *Courtesy Janet MacLeod, Adamant.*

Willey's Store in Greensboro after a new section was added to create a new business from the two former rival general stores. *Courtesy Greensboro Historical Society.*

Willey's Store (left) and its competitor in Greensboro sit side-by-side in the early 1930s. *Courtesy Greensboro Historical Society.*

Powers Market in North Bennington is a rare example of a country store in Greek Revival temple form with full-blown columned portico. The enclosure of the porch under the portico seems to be a twentieth-century alteration. *Courtesy Maria Scully, North Bennington.*

The vernacular architecture is spectacular. They go back and back and back, and keep going." They may drop downstairs to hardware or out back to feed or upstairs to hunting clothes, around the corner to wine and around another corner to guns or "looking eye-to-eye with a stuffed animal. They're an adventure."

Vernacular architecture puts a room or a window or a staircase where it is needed, not where architectural design suggests. Gary Lord finds it intriguing, as with Jericho Center, which "has the lines of an early nineteenth-century building, but the façade was extensively reworked in the late nineteenth century. The turned porch posts are of that era, as is the peculiar, idiosyncratic parapet with it hooded, bracketed and shingled—very Victorian."

Buildings may simply be rolled together, as with Willey's in Greensboro or the Wayside in West Arlington. Or stores may be classically placed in a brick block, as with F.H. Gillingham's in Woodstock. Metal or beaded ceilings came and went in Taftsville. An eight-sided window appeared in Jericho Center. Some may look strange in Vermont, such as the Greek Revival temple that is Powers Market in North Bennington.

the banks, there is an ugliness of discarded refrigerators and car husks, and a country store does not disguise its stark technology behind a wall. New cash registers, computers, lottery, video rentals and ATMs are up front beside racks of cigarettes and snack foods.

Wooden floors are not allowed in new stores, so some of the dirt in the cracks of the historic country stores might be from Ethan Allen's boots. But country stores are not museums, and their owners had to be fleet-footed to survive the successive pressures of supermarkets, convenience stores and big box stores. With the ATM and the wine department came the owner's need to learn a new vocabulary. The wheel of cheddar under a plastic hood became a case of artisanal farm cheeses. Once content to let go of their post offices, stores now demanded they stay—in Waterbury, East Montpelier, Glover, Taftsville, Benson, West Danville and many more.

"Stores are romantic sounding and looking, but very hard to run," says Hathaway. Past and present collide. The old way of inventory demanded that every article be counted; the inventory book listed each item, its sale price and the quantity on hand. Some storekeepers kept the entire inventory in their heads, and they would "clean store" shelf by shelf, wiping and replacing. Their knowledge of the inventory was so deep—and continues so in stores like Dan & Whit's and H.N. Williams—that a customer might ask for any item and the storekeeper would know if it was in stock, whether and when it was sold out or no longer made and

Baker's Store in North Ferrisburg (before the original "h" was restored to the name). There were several buildings that handled animal feed and automobile service. *Courtesy the Vermont Collection at Middlebury College Library.*

Vermont Studio Furniture occupies the remaining building of what was once Baker's Store in North Ferrisburgh. In 2008 the road is paved and the covered bridge is gone.

be able to walk up to the shelf and hand it to the customer. It continues into the days of barcodes and automated replenishment—without abating the grinding hours of 6:00 a.m. to 9:00 p.m.

Those who did not change failed once more, or continue to struggle. Change does not sit comfortably on the Vermont brow.

Interstates brought the population of 390,000 to 608,000 in forty years—a gain larger than Vermont's total growth since the War of 1812. The state's politics shifted and along with it came a deepening pride of place, reflected in 1970's Act 250. The most far-reaching environmental law in America, it was coupled with a renewed interest in historical preservation and an earnest if abortive back-to-the-land movement by young people, restraining rapacious corporate destruction of field, farm and country store. Vermont fought potential environmental and economic degradation, ultimately squeezing its first Wal-Mart into an existing building.

Yet the stores struggle. They have higher prices, even if their owners believe they are fair. Says Hathaway, "We *are* fair. And we're *there*. We *volunteer*. We participate in all areas of community. Formula stores do not. You don't know the owner, they're not in the community." Owners of country stores live above their stores, watching communities change from farming to second homes. Stores like H.N. Williams have survived for 170 years by learning to understand that change.

During the Great Depression, H.N. Williams Harness Shop equipped the local carriages as well as making bicycles and sleighs. *Courtesy Billy Brownlee, Dorset*.

H.N. Williams Store was finally on a well-traveled road by the 1930s, and had been transformed from harness shop to general store. *Courtesy Billy Brownlee, Dorset*.

The H.N. Williams Store in Dorset in the late twentieth century. It was lifted up and a full foundation was added that today includes a clothing showroom. *Courtesy Billy Brownlee, Dorset.*

In 2001, an organization was formed to help the country and general stores prosper in the twenty-first century, without losing their historical and community sense of place, and to sustain their living legacy of family and support of local producers. The Vermont Alliance of Independent Country Stores grew to more than fifty members, providing Internet presence and letting the storekeepers know they are not alone.

Generations of people have grown up with corner stores, country stores and general stores—as it is still in Vermont. As life becomes extreme, difficult and faster, Vermont's stores feel like museums and special places of the past, even as they are the "mine canaries" of warning. What will Vermont's future be like? Perhaps, as Charles Morrissey wrote of our woes, "Vermont isn't different enough."

In *Successful Calamity*, Edmund Fuller recounted his experiences living in a small 1950s Vermont town. It struck him that city and country people differ only in what they mask—country people are more direct and their beings exposed. Being in need and being able to help are two sides of the Vermont personality. The essence of the small town is found in human nature, not steel and glass and brick.

PART II

A Visitor's Guide to Vermont's Independent Country Stores

What's in a Country Store?

Vermont's independent country and general stores have a greater variety of goods and services than most city downtowns, shopping malls or big box stores. Read aloud, read quickly: You can find groceries and dry goods, local and fresh goods (baked, produce, soap, syrup, beers, dairy, Atlantic and local seafood), frozen goods, fresh pizza, ice, ice cream, creemies and cones, sundaes, a soda fountain, a deli and indoor restaurant or snack tables, chess and checkerboards set up, luxury goods (local and touristic, wine, beer, cigarettes, soda, snack foods, liquor, etc.), clothing (boots, coats, shoes, shirts; gift clothes, including t-shirts and hats), greeting and postcards, party supplies, sunglasses, hardware (small and large), paint, tools (shop and kitchen), plumbing supplies, small appliances, clocks, heaters, wood stoves, sugaring supplies, window glass, furniture, children's games,

The moose at Currier's Market in Glover greets patrons of the post office. Currier's has more than one hundred animals hunted in the local forest.

puzzles, books, school supplies, ATM, fax, video games, trading library, dry cleaning pickup, UPS/FedEx pickup, photocopying, a bus stop, catering, keys cut, photo processing, Internet access, public phone, tourist information, utility payments, weather reporting, bulletin boards, newspapers, magazines, maps, local promotions and tickets, money orders, local artwork, blown glass, carvings, candles, pottery, the lottery, a post office or letter drop, stamps, gift wrap, phone cards, stationery, notary and justice of the peace.

There's more: hunting and fishing licenses, guns, ammunition, meat dressing and cutting, bowhunting supplies, black powder supplies, buck knives, fishing rods and line, muzzleloading supplies, worms, game reporting, feed, harnesses, tack, vet supplies, pet food, a hitching post, gas, oil, diesel, kerosene, washer fluid, motor fluids, firewood, lanterns, batteries, flashlights, kindling, seeds, snow shovels, swimming supplies, private label goods, directions and *advice.*

Traveling in Vermont

Visitors who leave the interstates see the best of the region, but also confront Vermont's roads. State highways turn and twist, slowing to twenty-five miles per hour as they weave through villages, at the center of which are inevitably small stores with food, fuel and often souvenirs—as well as directions from Vermont's "unofficial welcome centers." With so few real welcome centers in Vermont, the unofficial ones, with local owners who know every inch of the nearby geography, are indispensable.

While following colorful local directions, travelers soon notice something else: dirt. As Tim Brookes wrote, "Nobody ever moved to Vermont because of its well-paved roads." When suburbia was reaching out of the cities in postwar America with asphalt, Vermont remained dirt. The first road in Vermont was paved in 1911 on the Theodor N. Vail estate in Lyndon, and since then it has been a slow and discontinuous process. As late as 1950, only a few major roads—U.S. Highways 2, 4, 5, 7 and 9, along with parts of Vermont 100, 103 and 105—were paved. The secondary roads were dirt, the side roads often bumpy tracks.

Sections of heavily traveled roads are increasingly paved to save maintenance expenses. Even so, fewer than half of Vermont's roads are paved today—7,030 miles—but 8,660 remain unpaved, including Vermont 65, which passes Allis State Park, rolling over Brookfield's Floating Bridge to join the high road south to Floyd's Store in Randolph Center.

For the unwary traveler, road maps can be deceptive. Heading from Vergennes to Panton, the author missed the Panton road on its blind curve, and started down West Street. A few hundred feet over the crest, it became a field of snow traversed only by snowmobiles; with no turnaround, backing up was the only option.

West Street was paved, as are the roads over some of the mountain gaps—but they are still closed in winter. Vermont has four grades of unpaved roads, along with the special classification of Ancient Roads. *Caveat conductor.*

Gravel roads are surfaced with crushed rock occasionally matted down by stone dust from local quarries; at the height of summer, these roads are smooth and often wide. Speed limits can be up to fifty miles per hour—and Vermonters may find even that speed sluggish, notwithstanding occasional cracked windshields.

Graded earth roads are similar to gravel, but without the hearty stone layer. Driving a graded road—smoothed by heavy equipment monthly or after a storm—requires care. It is dusty with loose and washboarded surfaces that can kick a car off the road, even at thirty-five miles per hour.

Unimproved/primitive roads vary by season. Low-slung cars will never survive these roads, which are traveled by farm and logging vehicles and local automobiles whose drivers know every rock and rut. Unimproved roads are sometimes tracks through grass and over runs of water, and you're guaranteed a long hike back in winter.

Untraveled roads are those which are no longer in vehicular use but haven't been "thrown up" by the town. They may actually be driveways where home owners enjoy the privilege of free winter snowplowing. Walk, don't drive.

But that's not all. Town highways are classified as 1, 2, 3, 4 or Legal Trail. If you're not sure, ask. The road to Northfield's scenic Slaughterhouse Covered Bridge is short but becomes Class 4 before a driver can turn around.

Driving in Vermont's snow is an exercise in adrenaline. Even interstate highways glaze over and cars head for the snowbanks, but local paved and dirt roads demand snow tires. Many roads close for the season—and snow season runs October through May. Closed roads don't mean "try me if you can." They mean "closed," because at the end of the road will be a mountain of snow dumped from the plowed section. You don't want to see that after ten hair-raising miles across Lincoln Gap.

The high road was the main route through Randolph Center from Royalton to Williamstown. Like every Vermont road of the day, it was unpaved. *Courtesy Al and Jan Floyd, Randolph Center.*

And then there's mud season. Classic photos show cars mired down to their chassis in mud. Travel became impossible during mud season—and remains so today. Frost is driven down into the soil during winter, rarely thawing during the long, deep winter months of late December through April. When the surface thaws in a sudden burst of spring weather, the water cannot drain, rocks float to the surface and stretches of land become mud bogs into which heavy vehicles balanced on skinny tires sink dramatically and irrevocably. With 55 percent of Vermont's roads unpaved, that's some 8,700 miles of mud—known as "rough sledding" in Vermont parlance.

Even the paved roads are cause for complaint, as in spring they grow dramatic frost heaves that push the asphalt up to suspension-snapping heights. The winter this book was being written was a ruin of asphalt roads, the worst in memory for the Vermont Department of Transportation.

Being Understood

Vermontean is not a foreign language, and most names are traditionally pronounced—Guilford, Randolph, Canaan— but twenty-five towns are a little odd. Learning to say unusual town names may get you there faster.

Adamant	A-d'MANT (*A* as in "habit," *MANT* as in "handle," with two equally accented syllables)
Albany	ALB'nee (*ALB* as in "Albert," not "All")
Athens	AYTH'ns or ATH'ns (the pronunciation depends on the speaker's age)
Barnard	BAR-n'rd
Barnet	BAR-nit
Barre	BARE-ee or BAR-ee (*BAR* as in "had")
Bomoseen	BO-m'seen
Calais	KAL-ess (*KAL* as in "calibrate")

Charlotte	sh'LOTT
Corinth	k'RINTH
Coventry	KAH-v'n-tree (*KAH* as in "odd")
Glover	GLUV'r
Goshen	GO-sh'n
Groton	GROTT'n
Houghtonville	HO'tn-ville
Lamoille	l'MOYL
Leicester	LESS-t'r
Moscow	MAHSS-ko
Orleans	or-LEENS
Pownal	POW-n'l
Quechee	KWEE-chee
Poultney	POLT-nee
Topsham	TOPS'm
Townshend	TOWNS'nd
Wolcott	WALL-kit
Worcester	WUSS-t'r (*WUSS* as in "put")

So if you are ready, here are the nine tours of Vermont's independent country stores. There are 275 country and general stores in Vermont. These sample tours include about 50 stores, but do not be afraid to explore the byways of Vermont.

WEST SIDE STORY

Massachusetts to Montréal via the Champlain Islands
(2 days, 280 miles)

Williamstown, Massachusetts—Pownal, Vermont—North
Bennington—West Arlington—Dorset (Williams)—Dorset
(Union)—Pawlet—Danby (or loop onto Tour 5 here)—
East Poultney—Castleton—Hydeville—Benson—Orwell—
Panton—Vergennes—North   Ferrisburgh—Charlotte—
Burlington
East Scenic Route to Saint Albans
West Scenic Route to South Hero—Grand Isle—North Hero
Meet at Alburgh—Rouses Point, New York—Montréal,
Québec, Canada

Pownal is on U.S. Route 7 just north of the Massachusetts
line from Williamstown. There's no country store in Pownal
these days—the S.L. Smith & Son Store is long gone, along

Alburgh

North Hero

Grande Isle

South Hero

Lake
Champlain

Burlington

Charlotte

North Ferrisburgh

Panton

Vergennes

I 89

22A

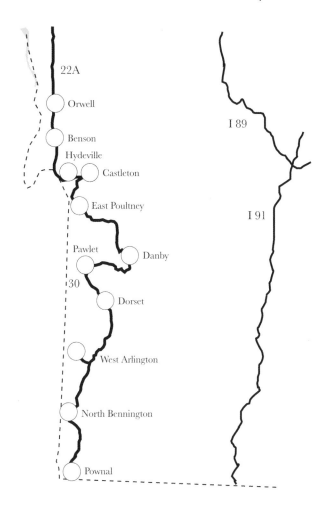

22A

Orwell

Benson

Hydeville

Castleton

East Poultney

Pawlet

Danby

30

Dorset

West Arlington

North Bennington

Pownal

I 89

I 91

with the town's three covered bridges—but it is a scenic start for a few days up along the soft western valleys of Vermont. Heading up U.S. Route 7 to Vermont 9 to Vermont 67A leads to North Bennington, where the remarkable architecture of the Powers Market can be seen: a Greek Revival temple with a columned portico that started as a company store in 1833 for the Thatcher & Welling Paper Mill.

The path to West Arlington's store is from U.S. Route 7 to the historic route Vermont 7A, and westward onto Vermont 313. Four miles from the intersection is the Wayside Country Store.

Several country stores began life as harness shops. The blacksmiths, wheelwrights and harness makers provided movement to travel into and through towns. Wayside Country Store in West Arlington was built in the 1850s and opened as a saddle and harness shop in 1860. The railroads did not come to the town, so the shop continued until it became a general store in 1879. Prior to that year, another store operated about a mile away, just before the turn to the West Arlington covered bridge, among a group of homes known as the Huddle.

The two stores were both small, and it was not long before the Hurd Store was jacked up and rolled on logs up the hill to the harness shop, where the two buildings were joined, becoming the town's new general store. It operated through the 1920s as a store and trading post until the Smith family bought it and made it Smith's Cash Store, operating and even expanding through the Great Depression.

Raymond Smith's grandfather ran the business until 1954, with his living quarters in the center section between the original two buildings. His mother's kitchen was in the back. Spring water fed the store from 1,800 feet back and up the hill, and the taps ran all winter to keep them from freezing.

Smith's Cash Store had gas pumps, sold machinery parts and bought animal skins and wool. Wagonloads of sheared wool would arrive and be weighed on a scale built into the road, now paved over with Vermont Route 313. The store was a post office, and had exotic items such as lead-lined boxes of tea from China. During Prohibition, the family made home-brew—keeping lookout through a peephole in the back door.

Like most country stores, Smith's kept years of unsold goods. From hatpins to high-button shoes, the building was packed full of useful but out-of-fashion items. The Second World War was over, and Ray Smith's father had a plan to clear out the stock from *both* wars. He began sales in 1947, and then came up with an idea. If he gave away money, people would come right back to spend it—the piles of old stock would be gone, the customers would take it away for him and he would get the money back. But how to give away the money?

Thomas Rockwell, the middle son of artist Norman Rockwell, lived in town and photographed the famous

Smith's Cash Store in 1949 during the great clearance sale, when chickens with money were tossed from the roof to a waiting crowd eager for cash and dinner. *Thomas Rockwell; courtesy Raymond Smith, West Arlington.*

sale. Thirteen-year-old Raymond Smith stood on the porch roof with his father and store employees. Chickens had been brought upstairs with one- and five-dollar bills tied to their legs. They were carried through the windows and tossed from the porch over the heads of the excited crowd for the customers to chase. The "flying chickens" sale gave people money and goods—and fresh chicken for dinner!

Today the gas pumps are gone, but the store stands otherwise unchanged, save for a coat of paint and the

Save for the ATM on the left, this 2008 scene of the cluttered roll-top desk at the Wayside Store in West Arlington might be from a century ago.

westernmost windows replaced with shelves. Doug and Nancy Tschorn bought it in 1984, renaming it Wayside Country Store.

The Tschorns were optimistic. Perhaps they would only sell a few cans of pork and beans and some sporting goods, recalls Doug Tschorn. But trade picked up and the store expanded. Twelve miles was a long way to go for a few grocery items, so the store's coffee and conversation table with mounted deer head above—even without a cracker barrel—was popular. Wayside became a social meeting place.

Smith's Cash Store in 1950, painted white and with living quarters in the store's center section; the right-hand section was once the Hurd Store, moved from a mile away. *Courtesy Nancy Tschorn, West Arlington.*

Politicians would show up, petitions for elective office or wilderness preservation would appear. Raymond Smith would pop in every morning. "Most of the world's problems get solved right here, but there's nobody listening to us, so they don't take action on them," Smith says.

Today, Doug Tschorn guides the store from his cluttered roll-top desk, counts up an inventory of nearly fifteen thousand items and happily takes visitors on a store tour. He randomly rattles off contents. It's a catchall for UPS and FedEx. People

The Wayside Country Store in 2008, now painted red and with living quarters upstairs. The windows in the right-hand section have been replaced with shelves of goods.

leave packages. Here are the fax and copy machines for store and public. Postcards and greeting cards. Local ice cream, local milk. Handmade jewelry. Mason jars. Brooms. Rakes. Glassware. Maps. Frozen food. Spam. Rhubarb wine. "We're more than a supermarket," he says with pride. "We combine a little from every department store. These days a big box store can be condensed into one aisle of a country store!" He continues. Produce, local. Mushrooms, bananas, green peppers, celery, apples, grapefruit, avocados. Seeds. Electrical goods. Car air fresheners. Pesto and sauces. Chocolate fudge sauce. Batteries. Flashlights. All maple products—100 percent Vermont. Salt licks. Grass seed. Health and beauty aids. Home remedies. Bunion cushions. Nail clippers. T- and sweatshirts, special for the store.

And then there comes that line again: "If we don't have it, you don't need it."

Backtracking from the Wayside to Vermont 7A, you travel north to Vermont 30 and the village of Dorset, which has two very different businesses: a true village store and a true country store—the Dorset Union Store and H.N. Williams.

Father and son craft tack at the H.N. Williams Store in Dorset, which has remained in the family since it was founded in the 1840s. *Courtesy Billy Brownlee, Dorset.*

The Franklin Hotel in Pawlet was a great Federal-style stone building in the touristic heyday. Today it is Machs' General Store—with a tree in the middle. *Courtesy Marilyn Bellemare, Pawlet.*

The latter comes up first on the ride north, an unassuming building with a simple white sign and small front door. Inside, the contents of this 1840 business range from a room of Vermont food products to animal feed, seasonal clothing, hunting and fishing supplies, sugaring equipment, dry goods and hardware. Williams is one of the few stores that serves an entire community clientele, whether they are preparing for winter or repairing the barn, making breakfast or planting the herb garden, fixing the car or getting ready for vacation. If it is a quiet moment—which it rarely is in

Machs' General Store in Pawlet is largely unchanged. Even though the Federal-style lintels appear to be gone, they are merely painted over.

any country store—ask proprietor Billy Brownlee for a peek at the twenty-two-inch virgin softwood planks that make up the attic ceiling.

In town on the green is the Dorset Union Store, formerly Peltier's Market. This 1816 building is a classic, with white clapboards, pitched roof and dark green shutters; in summer, the storekeeper rolls out the awnings for the perfect New England scene. Inside the Dorset Union are rooms of goods, feed, dry goods and wine, and a coffee bar. Exploring the long, narrow store is time well spent.

From Dorset, Vermont 30 winds north to Pawlet and a crossroads in the Mettowee Valley with a looming stone building—Machs' Store. Originally the Franklin Hotel, it was built in 1808; John Mach established the store in 1945, with it changing hands again in 2002. Machs' spans Flower Brook and has a box built into the floor with tree, brook and waterfall visible from inside the store.

Turning onto and following Vermont 133 brings a musicians' haven, the Danby Four Corners Store, into view. Along with gas, groceries, newspapers, shoes and clothing, the store also sells and trades guitars, fiddles, banjos, basses, mandolins and resonator guitars.

Head north until Vermont 140 comes into sight, and then northwest through Middletown Springs—where gas is available at Grant's Village Store—and onward to East Poultney, birthplace of *New York Times* founder George Jones and *New York Herald Tribune* founder Horace Greeley. With the post office inside, along with animal feed and fresh-baked goods, East Poultney General Store can be a busy place for locals. Visitors stand on the bridge that overlooks the gorge and waterfalls of the Poultney River.

From Vermont 140 again joining Vermont 30, it's a short ride to Vermont 4A and the busy Castleton National Historic District and the Village Store. The store is a modest, classic wood-frame building, a store since the mid-nineteenth century, built new after the former building and several others were razed by fire in 1890. Present owners

Pam and John Rehlen purchased the Ballard Store in 1971 and it became Castleton Village Store. Pam's family has lived in town—home to the oldest college in Vermont—for six generations.

Castleton is a study in the effects of growth. The store used to house a post office and soda fountain, but these fell to progress. U.S. Route 4, the main east-west highway from New York, passed in front of the store, where Castleton joined three gas stations and many other businesses in a vibrant economic community. But on July 4, 1971, Independence Day also celebrated the opening of the Route 4 Bypass. Traffic dropped, Rehlen explains, but at the same time quality of village life, including its pedestrian characteristics, improved. The village was reoriented toward local people, with less transient traffic. Grocery and hardware were added in the mid-1970s, but larger chain stores opened around the same time. Mini-marts pressured the store as they grew in number from three to eleven in a few years. Groceries, magazines, newspapers, gifts and wine were expanded, but hardware was gone. Brands vanished.

Today, Castleton Village Store has one of Vermont's best wine shops, an extensive Vermont cheese department with a large selection of the state's artisanal cheeses and native grass-fed beef and pork from the nearby Wing Farm. And not to be missed across the street from the village store is the 1940s-era Silk City Diner, now restored as the Birdseye Diner.

Just two miles from Castleton Vermont 4A is Harbor View General Store in Hydeville. On the western shore of Lake Bomoseen, it is a classic grocery and supply stop for those heading to fish, canoe, water-ski, kayak or boat on the lake—or just sit and talk in the Adirondack chairs on the porch. The store carries Vermont specialty products, locally made gift items, t-shirts and sweatshirts, campers' supplies, fishing tackle, honey, maple syrup, penny candy, homemade pastries and daily specials.

A turn onto Vermont 22A heads toward the tiny village of Benson. The welcoming clapboarded store at the center has an equally tiny collection of every item a local customer might want—as well as the local post office. It has to be well stocked, as the next closest store is eight miles away in Fair Haven. Local resident Wesley Chandler, who was born in Benson in 1933 as one of thirteen siblings, recalls that the village once had a hardware store, three hotels and three country stores where bread was five cents and cornmeal thirty-five cents for one hundred pounds. Benson was a main stage stop from New York to Montréal.

Continuing northward on the highway leads to a right turn on Vermont 73 to Orwell and Buxton's Store. On the right side of the town square, not far from the last stronghold of British and German troops during the American Revolution at Mount Independence, is the one-hundred-year-old Buxton's. This is the beginning of fertile farm country, and Buxton's carries the feed and food for beast and farmer—and also for the bikers who frequent the store. The First National Bank of Orwell, frontier-town brick with "teller bars," is one of the last privately held national banks in the United States, joined by the Congregational church and its typical white spire and the elementary school that absorbed the old town hall. Buxton's was purchased in 2006 by the Edwards family from Dick and Thelma Buxton, who ran it for forty-one years.

Back on Vermont 22A, the next thirty miles north to Panton pass through the small towns of Shoreham, Bridport and Addison, where a turn left on Vermont 17 ends at Lake Champlain. South to the early French settlement of Chimney Point goes to New York; north along Lake Street leads to Panton and Andy Mégroz's Panton General Store, built 175 years ago as a surgeon's residence. In 1908 it became a general store. Once the Panton Store had a post office, where the postmistress, unable to read, sorted mail by color on her quilt. From the door, sixty-five miles of mountain ranges stretch out, protected by federal flyway, wildlife preserve and farms. "You don't feel claustrophobic here," explains Mégroz.

During the summer in Panton, the Basin Harbor Club has been run for a century by the same family. Button Bay State Park, River's Edge Campground, Benedict Arnold's boat launch in Arnold Bay and the Maritime Museum are all nearby.

Leaving Panton east passes through Vergennes, Vermont's first city ("Smallest City in the U.S.A."), an old railroad town featuring fine dining and an opera house, and diverse architecture—Greek Revival, Italianate, Neoclassical Revival, Georgian mansions and a Gothic church. A turn onto 22A to U.S. Route 7 north leads to a right-turn side trip to North Ferrisburgh (the "h" in most "burgh" towns was removed by the U.S. Post Office but restored in recent times). In North Ferrisburgh is the remnant of a country store—Baker's Store, a brick building that sat at the outlet of a covered bridge in the early part of the twentieth century. Today the building is intact and beautifully preserved as the home of Vermont Studio Furniture.

Back on U.S. Route 7 and up to Vermont F5 in Charlotte is found the Old Brick Store, built about 1840. Near covered bridges in Prindlee Road, hiking on Mount Philo, biking at Demeter Park, sailing on Lake Champlain, flea markets in town, berry picking at Pelkey's and a ferry to New York, the Old Brick Store is a community meeting point. Its comfortable porch welcomes locals and visitors alike, and the busy lakeside community contrasts with the wide open farmland to the south.

It is twelve miles up the road to Burlington, but a side jog via Interstate 189 to 89 north gets out of the congestion for the next leg, either east or west.

The eastern route exits I-89 at St. Albans, a historic rail town that is the northern terminus of the Central Vermont Railway, site of a Confederate raid in 1864 (via Canada!) and the home of the Center Market, an urban general store.

After St. Albans, roads north eventually lead to Swanton and toward the Champlain Islands, Alburgh, Rouses Point in New York, and I-87 to Montréal.

The western route exits at U.S. Route 2 west toward the Champlain Islands, through South Hero and the Keeler Bay Variety Store, Grand Isle, North Hero and Hero's Welcome General Store, Alburgh, Rouses Point in New York and I-87 to Montréal.

TOUR 2.

East Side Kids

Massachusetts to Canada along the Connecticut
(1–2 days, 255 miles)

Bernardston, Massachusetts—Guilford, Vermont—
Putney—Saxtons River—Grafton—Chester—Norwich (or
loop onto Tour 3 here)—Bradford—Newbury—Peacham
(or loop onto Tour 6 via West Danville, or Tour 9
via Wells River)—Danville—Lyndonville—East Burke—
Island Pond—Bloomfield via Brighton State Park—West
Charleston—Derby Line—Québec, Canada

The businesses in southeastern Vermont are attuned to
travelers. U.S. Route 5 from the Massachusetts border
travels eight miles to the artistic center of Guilford, where
the Guilford Country Store combines Vermont products,
wines, cheeses and a computer outlet. The store was built
as a tavern in 1817, becoming a country store in the 1930s.

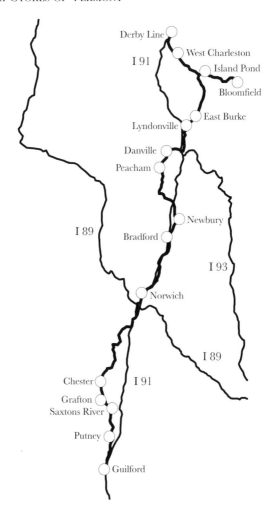

Derby Line

West Charleston

Island Pond

Bloomfield

I 91

East Burke

Lyndonville

Danville

Peacham

Newbury

Bradford

I 89

I 93

Norwich

I 89

Chester

I 91

Grafton

Saxtons River

Putney

Guilford

Guilford, chartered with a New Hampshire grant in 1754, was an early settlement defended in the 1780s by Ethan Allen during the "Guilford War."

Up U.S. Route 5 from Guilford is Putney, an artistic community with a storied history. Mast timber for the British Royal Navy was harvested there in the 1730s. The town was chartered in 1753, electrified as early as 1914 and is today the site of the Yellow Barn Music Festival. The Putney General Store was built as a gristmill in 1769, becoming a store on the Post Road in 1843 and continuing in operation as Chandler & Keyes, Corser Store, S.L. Davis Store, Cummings Store, Fickett's General Store and finally the Putney General Store. Inside are a deli and café, meat counter and Vermont fresh and packaged products, plus ice cream, coffee and wine—with a second floor dedicated to games, puzzles and souvenirs.*

Leaving Route 5 for Vermont 121 enters the southern sheltered mountains. The first stop is Saxtons River, population five hundred, in Vermont's Pleasant Valley, with an academy and a playhouse, a baseball team and a white-steepled church—and the Saxtons River Village Market.

Vermont 121 to 35 arrives in Grafton, with a worthwhile stop at the Grafton Village Cheese Company and the forty-

---

*Fire continues to change store histories. Putney General Store burned to the ground on May 4, 2008, the day this book went into production. See page 69.

six-room Old Tavern Inn, and continues up the Chester Road into Chester Depot, home of Lisai's Chester Market. This store has undergone growth and accompanying alteration, revealing Vermont's frugal and practical nature before it embarked on its historical preservation movement of the 1970s. From the outside, Lisai's looks like it might be part of a city neighborhood—unremarkable, old and gray. But its story reaches back to the Green Mountain Turnpike, beside which the store was built in 1849 by Coleman Saunders at the same time the Rutland Railroad was arriving in the area, following the turnpike route. Saunders left the grocery for a lumber business in Grafton and Chester, and sold the store to Fred A. Leland in 1892, who expanded the grocery with fruit, tobacco, cigars, candy, medicines, extracts, cured meats and teas, along with a soda fountain. Leland's store grew from a tidy cottage and stable to a display-front building, and under Hugh Jameson, who reopened the store after a brief closure during World War II, to a tall structure with lifted ceiling. Because of its owners' practical response to changing markets, architectural experts aren't fond of this store—but the locals have been happy to be able to fulfill all their needs in one place for over a century and a half.

Not far from the store is Stone Village, built from the gneiss quarried in the area that make the site a visitor's wonder; today, the trains still pass the Chester store, with the Green Mountain Railroad running freight and, during foliage season, tourists. The newly renovated station sits

Before the days of automated crossings, "Look Out for the Engine" was the only warning offered to carriages and riders. *Courtesy Lisai's Market, Chester.*

"Look Out for the Engine" is gone, but automated signals warn of the train that still passes along the present-day Green Mountain Railroad.

Dan & Whit's store in Norwich makes no effort to appeal to Vermont's pastoral image, instead offering a storewide bulletin board for local residents.

beside Vermont 103, where cars and trucks make it a heavily traveled route through the state's south central mountains.

Onward from Chester is the forty-five-mile country route to Norwich: Vermont 103 to 10 toward North Springfield, 106 through Perkinsville to 44 toward Brownsville and then passing 12 through Hartland Four Corners to U.S. Route 5 past White River Junction, with a quick left into town toward Dan & Whit's. You will want to stop.

There were four general stores in Norwich by 1800, and L.K. Merrill opened another store in 1891—the one that

The basement of Dan & Whit's store in Norwich is filled with wood that will be used to heat the vast general store all the long winter. There is no other source of heat.

would become Dan & Whit's. The Merrill family ran the store, with Whit Hicks joining the staff in 1932 and Dan Fraser in 1933. The pair bought the store in 1955, making additions in 1963, 1968 and 1972, and adding a copper roof in 1988. The store kept its feet in both past and future, heating exclusively with wood to this day, but installing computers as early as 1991.

Dan & Whit's is not handsome, but it is solid. Covered with a storewide bulletin board, the store is disguised behind an asphalt parking lot, gas pumps, FedEx drop and Coke machine, and surrounded by the stately contours of the Norwich Inn and the Congregational church. Inside the store, the cluttered outside drops away for an even more cluttered interior, crowded with customers for fourteen hours a day, and where a rack of shelves holds newspapers reserved for individual patrons. Flowers sit next to hardware, toys by boots and shoes, glassware by rakes and garden tools, garden decorations and birdbaths by canning goods and rolls of fencing. Groceries, souvenirs and every item to serve town and country are stocked. The basement is filled with a dozen neatly stacked woodpiles, where cord after cord is burned by three huge wood furnaces.

Their website declares, "You haven't shopped at Dan & Whit's long enough if…" and lists twenty-nine items, including "You call on holidays to see if we are open," "Mike doesn't know what kind of car you drive and the names of all your dogs," "You try to use a credit card in the express lane," "You are used to paying $2.50 for a cup of coffee" and "You wonder why the wood stove works when the power is out." Young Dan Fraser now runs the store, and he will be happy to greet you from behind his shop apron.

The long trip up Route 5 arrives next in Bradford after passing Thetford—an interesting side trip for its lovely village green—and Fairlee, with a pleasant lake to visit in summer. The Bliss Village Store is found in the center of the Bradford Village Historic District, where the Connecticut and Passumpsic Rivers Railroad (later the Boston & Maine) once came through the village. The Bliss Store is the former Bliss Hotel, a clapboarded, two-and-a-half-story Greek Revival building dating from 1806, with an unusual two-story portico with a balcony and pedimented gable above. Inside, it is a complete latter-day general store, with groceries, baked goods and souvenirs.

The next stop along Route 5 is Newbury, with its striking 1840 Newbury Village Store—another Greek Revival temple form with a recessed porch in the pediment. Gary Lord explained that "the broad, flat, surfaces are typical of the austerity of the style; robust and well articulated." It is as picture-postcard as the town itself.

Sliding off U.S. Route 5 to Vermont 25 leads through East Corinth to Waits River and its country store (see Tour 3 for more on Waits River), to U.S. Route 302 east to Groton, where the country store is now closed, and up the Peacham Road to Peacham (see Tour 9 for more on the Peacham Store, and here you can loop onto Tour 6 via West Danville, or Tour 9 via Wells River) to Danville, where its country store is also closed, joining U.S. Route 2 east through the two historic towns of St. Johnsbury and Lyndonville. A stop in either town for lunch or dinner is welcome.

The mid-1800s were a time of flourishing trade for St. Johnsbury, where Thaddeus Fairbanks invented the platform scale and his family became the town's chief employer and benefactor. The Athenaeum is a nineteenth-century art gallery, and the Fairbanks Museum houses an observatory and peculiarly personal science collections. Some will remember St. Johnsbury as the shooting location for *Where the Rivers Flow North*, *The Spitfire Grill* and *Disappearances*. Lyndonville is the other side of "Saint J"—a working-class town with a nearby state college and rows of small businesses. It is not promoted as a touristic town, so a visit will be a more authentic Vermont experience, including stops at the Shores Memorial Museum and its photo collection and extensive projects via the "Living History Classroom."

Vermont 114 leads to East Burke and Bailey's & Burke, a general store that has expanded into a community hub. East Burke is one of Vermont's truly small villages, blessed with the East Branch of the Passumpsic River that was for many years its income during log drives, and cursed by the same river whose flooding would sweep down the main street—including the night before the author arrived.

With the storekeeper at Bailey's & Burke very busy cleaning up after the flood, Charlotte Downes, East Burke librarian, spoke about the store founded by pharmacist H.D. Webster in 1897. She recalled the pride and skill exhibited by Guy Poisson, who worked for storekeeper Floy Gibson in the 1930s. He would mark the price of each item as he put it in a paper bag, keeping track and writing down the total when he was done. "It was just this nice way of doing business," says Charlotte. "We used to charge penny candy for two cents, and then my father would come on Saturday and pay for it. Floy had a big roll-top desk by the wood-burning stove, and she would sit there and total up her money. They didn't have stacks of money, though."

Oddly, Floy kept pictures of the Dionne quintuplets on the wall. "She had them for every year as they were growing up. They were the ones that everyone noticed when you would come in the store." At the time, there were three stores in town, one with supplies such as sap buckets and wool clothes. Across the street was "a step up from the general store" with long counters, clothing material and some groceries. Finally, the general store had everything else, including garden tools, feed and harnesses.

In 1927 came the great flood that affected all of New England. "It took the mill. The river went down the street. It took all the dirt away. You couldn't get across the road it was so deep." And then in 2008, "the ice got clogged under the bridge and backed up, and the water was coming down so fast it finally broke through the side of the river and went out onto the road. It did it just like that."

There have been several owners since Floy. After she died, her nephew ran the store, later selling it to Jean Bailey, who created crafts and gifts in the 1970s, transforming it into an original country store in 1986. Jody Fried purchased the store in 1999, along with a cow barn and several other buildings, creating Bailey's & Burke as it is today, with a restaurant and pub, day-care center, real estate agency, eight residential apartments and a country store with groceries and Vermont products as well as baskets, woolen clothing and a wine cellar.

Also in East Burke is the White School Museum, an 1818 one-room schoolhouse containing original furniture, household items and hand tools.

Sixteen miles on Vermont 114 and three on Vermont 105 lead to Island Pond, home of the first International Railroad Junction in the country, where the ghosts of railroad men, lumberjacks and millworkers whisper on the wind, replaced by the farmers, hunters, bikers and visitors of today. Island Pond is a perfect example of Vermont's Northeast Kingdom geography and its undiscovered secrets.

Leaving Brighton State Park and continuing east on Vermont 105 brings the visitor to Vermont 102, where the road turns north around the Connecticut River, now slender and quiet not far from its Canadian source. The valley widens as the road arrives at the Debanville Store in Bloomfield, a small stop for lunch at one of its four tables, supplies for hunting and fishing and snacks and drinks for the rest of the day's travel.

For those looking for more activity, a drive back past Island Pond soon arrives via Vermont 105 in East and West Charleston and Derby, with excellent country stores in each, joining U.S. Route 5 toward the unique town of Derby Line. Combining the culture and architecture of two countries, Derby Line is the home of the Haskell Library and Opera House, where the international border between the United States and Canada runs through the middle of the 1901 Neoclassical building with stained-glass windows and a lustrous wooden interior. The stage is in Canada, and a black diagonal line is painted on the floor of the audience seats, making it possible to listen to European classical music while sitting in two North American countries at once.

GRANITE/VALLEY LOOP

Newbury to Norwich and back
(1 day, 110 miles)

Newbury—Bradford—Waits River—Graniteville—Barre—
Chelsea—South Strafford—Norwich—Newbury

This short loop is a day of varying scenery and eight unique towns. Follow U.S. Route 5 to visit Newbury and Bradford (for descriptions of Newbury and Bradford, see Tour 2), and turn east onto Vermont 25 to Waits River, one of the most photographed and painted villages in Vermont, considered special because of its visual symmetry.

The Waits River General Store is an example of persistence and imagination. The store first opened on the site in 1855, when it served as a stagecoach stop, hotel, company store and general store. The original building was destroyed by fire in 1953 and was rebuilt as a more modest

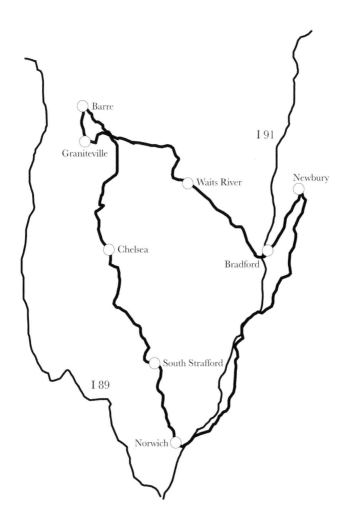

Barre

Graniteville

I 91

Waits River

Newbury

Chelsea

Bradford

South Strafford

I 89

Norwich

cottage in 1955. Bill MacDonald, the store's present owner, calls the area "sub-rural," where up to 90 percent of the business is local—meaning Waits River General provides groceries, feed and grain, pizza, cigarettes, beer and wine, propane refills, game reporting, a hitching post and, of course, a community bulletin board. He initiated a student encouragement program, providing pizzas for good grades.

Vermont 25 north to U.S. 302 and west moves from open rural to forested land, passing the reservoir that serves Barre and offers a nesting area for loons. A left onto Vermont 110 rises to Washington Heights, after which point eagle eyes will follow the signs to Graniteville, which, true to its name, was central to dozens of quarries at the turn of the twentieth century. After a stop for snacks at the Graniteville General Store—the modern survivor of a quarry company store, tall and narrow like mill stores everywhere in New England—the road winds west toward Rock of Ages and its extensive granite finishing works, museum and quarry bus tours. The bus tour is exciting, bouncing along rutted truck roads to the edge of the deep operations with startlingly tall cranes and cutting equipment in constant operation. Inside the finishing shed, also open to the public, the fifteen-foot diamond blades are at work slicing the granite. Rough granite souvenirs can be snagged from the slag heap, or finished ones from the museum shop.

From Vermont 110 a steep hill leads to a right turn onto Vermont 14, a short ride that includes a changing landscape

Before it was lost to fire, the Waits River General Store included the store, a gas station, barn and living quarters. A wood mill is to the right and a fire watchtower is behind. *Courtesy Bill MacDonald, Waits River.*

The Waits River General Store of 2008 has replaced the classic building lost to fire, but it maintains the same wide stock of goods.

from rural to suburban to the small urban character of Barre, "Granite Capital of the World" and erstwhile railroad center. Just past the interstate access road (locally called "the Beltway") is Dente's Market, another modest general store (its nomadic history is told in the "Quarries" section), but storekeeper Rick Dente happily recounts his family's long tenure in Barre to visitors.

Tracing back on U.S. 302 to Vermont 110 and continuing southward leads through Washington to Chelsea, a shire town—county seat in American parlance—with its two village greens. Notable in Chelsea are its old brick buildings in a vernacular Federal style, including Will's Store.

A well-preserved exterior with parapet gables, the building has a fanlight and splayed lintels above the windows—all characteristic of the Federal style in Vermont. It was leased to numerous owners. Perley Jones operated it, and Alonzo Powers briefly leased it in 1870 before Jones switched the lease to the father-son partnership Amos and William Hood, who sold drugs, patent medicines, groceries and "notions." Jones's survivors sold the building to the Hoods, including the son from Lowell, Massachusetts, who made Hood's Sarsaparilla. In 1875, it also became Hira Bixby's photo studio—with a skylight cut for him—succeeded later by Arthur Morey. William Hood took over for his father as a druggist, working in the store until 1912, when it was leased to Guy Buck. When Buck left for Northfield in 1923, Archie and Lena Bailey moved from Burke to take over.

The stress of being a storekeeper is evident on the face of Archie Bailey at A.H. Bailey's in Chelsea, now Will's Store. *Courtesy Will Gilman, Chelsea.*

The Baileys' store survived the great fire of 1926, but Lena soon relocated with her patent medicines, novelties, tobacco, ice cream, cards, gifts, needles, thread, ribbons, cloth, embroidery and crocheting. Fred Dickinson took over the operation of the Baileys' drugstore, bringing in ice cream machinery in 1945—a machine still used today under Will Gilman's tenure.

There are two ways to get from Chelsea to South Strafford—winter and summer. For the winter, follow Vermont 110 to Vermont 14, south and then east via

Vermont 132. In summer, turn east on the Strafford Road and over the hill. Both will lead to Coburn's General Store on a quiet turn in the road. A nineteenth-century home cottage with a latter-day portico and columns, Coburn's has extensions on either side that obscure its classic lines…but not its classic country store character. Coburn's has a tiny post office with about three hundred boxes, a full line of groceries and baked goods, shelves of hardware and plumbing supplies, t- and sweatshirts, gloves and farm goods. With no major shopping or gas nearby, Coburn's is a gathering place for the community.

The tour loops back through Norwich via Vermont 132 east, either directly to U.S. Route 5 or via a northward detour to the elegant green in Thetford. Vermont greens were not English commons, but were developed by churches as part of the landscape, with a focal point on the church; Thetford is an ideal example. After a visit to Dan & Whit's in Norwich, the tour ends again where it began, in Newbury. (For a description of Norwich and Newbury, see Tour 2.)

Central Vermont
Ski and Tree Loop

New York to Sugarbush to Burlington
(1–3 days, 210–230 miles)

New York State—Fair Haven, Vermont—Hydeville—
Castleton—Rutland—Mendon—(side trip to Pittsford)—
Pittsfield—Rochester— Hancock— Ripton—Lincoln—Warren
Adventurous trek to Roxbury—Northfield Falls
Timid trek to Waitsfield
Meet in Waterbury Center—Stowe (Shaw's)—Morrisville—
Elmore
Stop at Eden
Or back down to Jeffersonville—Fairfax—Burlington

On their way to a foliage tour or ski week, visitors arriving
in Vermont from the west to Rutland may bypass some
delightful villages and their stores. This central Vermont
ski and tree loop follows highways and byways through

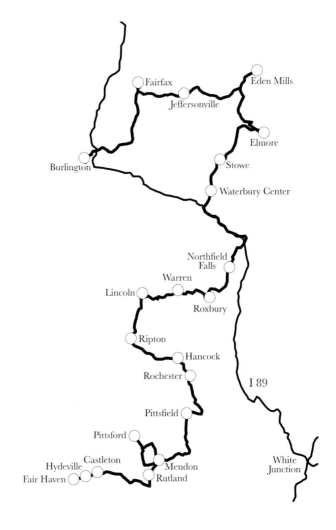

more than a dozen of them. On entering Vermont, pick up Vermont 22A/4A to Hydeville and the Harbor View General Store, then Vermont 4A eastward to the Castleton Village Store. (For a description of Hydeville and Castleton, see Tour 1.) Entering one of Vermont's industrial cities comes next, following 4A to Business 4 through center Rutland, where marble finishing sheds on both sides of the highway can be seen—and visited, so don't be shy. The touch of freshly polished marble is entrancing.

Business 4 passes through a renovated downtown and joins U.S. Routes 4 and 7, where a sharp dogleg at the north end of town carries Route 4 eastward and Route 7 northward. Nine miles north will offer a stop at Pittsford, where Kamuda's Country Store is found, along with the nearby Vermont Maple Museum and four covered bridges: Depot, Hammond, Gorham and Cooley. Kamuda's has a sandwich named for each, along with a buffet and deli.

Tracing back from Pittsford to the junction, Route 4 begins its slow eastward rise to Mendon Mountain. On the left—it takes a sharp eye—is the Mendon Country Store, a revived business that once served a mountain community and today is home to Vermont's largest collection of handmade gift baskets, samplers, bowls, boards, specialty foods, folk art, collectibles and homemade baked goods.

Continuing up the steep U.S. Route 4 passes the Killington Ski Area, local tourist stops and the left turn onto Vermont 100 toward the state's picturesque, forested and mountainous interior. A leisurely ride arrives at Pittsfield and the Original General Store—a business that was in danger of closing until an investor and his manager arrived.

The Pittsfield General Store had served the local five-hundred-person community since the 1880s, but by the beginning of the twenty-first century it was struggling opposite a convenience store on the touristic Vermont 100. Wall Street trader Joe DeSena acquired the store, changed the name to Vermont General Store and hired Michal Kukola to manage—

A transformed business is in Pittsfield, where the Original General Store has installed a wood-fired brick bread oven.

In a nod to European tradition, the Original General Store in Pittsfield opened a wine-tasting room in the twenty-first century.

Carefully tended jars of penny candy sit alongside a variety of Vermont local products at Pittsfield's Original General Store.

from New York via Moravian town Veselí nad Moravou. The transformation of the store from traditional country store to a modern business that serves locals and visitors was a rough ride, largely because monied investors are viewed with suspicion in rural Vermont. It took a few years for everyone to get acquainted, as well as a battle with the corporate Vermont Country Store, whose trademark policing pressured DeSena to change the name once again, to the Original General Store.

A wood-fired brick oven was installed, the store acquired an upright piano, a large deli was opened, additional rooms were made into inviting public spaces and a very European wine cellar was built with a spiral staircase and soft lighting. Vermont products line the shelves, from penny candy through fancy-grade maple syrup, and the store offers coffee and breakfast that have made its local name. Of critical importance for local residents has been saving the store and restoring it to its original nineteenth-century appearance.

Following Vermont 100 north takes the route through Gaysville, Stockbridge and Jerusalem into Rochester, home of the Quarry Hill Creative Center, Vermont's oldest alternative living community—often called "the Commune." Moving onward into Hancock and a left turn at Vermont 125 offers a visit to Hubbard's General Store, called by one writer "a real backwoods Mom & Pop store." The area is cool in summer, so after leaving Hubbard's, park and hike to Texas Falls.

What happens next depends on the season and the desire. In summer, continue on Vermont 125 or return to Vermont 100, which is the road to Granville and its sultry Granville Reservation State Park and twisting road through the Granville Gulf and Moss Glen Falls (on an east curve and easy to miss), a welcome respite. In winter, though, the next stop is Warren.

In summer, you can also stay on Vermont 125 to Ripton. Were it not for Robert Frost, Ripton might just be a bend in the road. It *is* a bend in the road, but also the place where Frost established the Breadloaf Writers' Conference. Stopping at the Ripton Country Store will by now become familiar—a small post office, barrels of onions, shelves of Vermont products, a comfortable sitting area and a display of product boxes stocked by the store fifty years ago. In summer, the wooden bench on the porch is the place to visit with regulars, after which you can hike the Robert Frost Trail.

A right turn at East Middlebury onto Vermont 116 to Vermont 17 through Bristol becomes a drive over the steep Lincoln Gap that will test a vehicle's pickup—and its brakes. A stop at the Lincoln General Store is in order, as well as one at the top of the gap in autumn that will reward you with brilliant foliage, gentle breezes and a grand vista. Continuing down Lincoln Gap is for the brave, as the steep grade twists and turns, sans guard rails and with barely room for two vehicles. At the bottom of the hill and through the covered bridge, cross Vermont 100 and slide into the sheltered village of Warren, where the old Warren Store is open seven days a week. A skiers' paradise in winter, the store also serves the local community and camp, supplying condo and second-home owners with Vermont foods, fresh baked goods and wines, as well as clothing and jewelry. Across the street is the Alta Day Spa and the Pitcher Inn (which was on fire as of this writing), and returning to the main road, one can travel to the major central Vermont ski areas in Warren, Waitsfield and Fayston. But the greater adventure is the trek over Roxbury Gap.

For the less adventurous, following Vermont 100 to Waitsfield arrives at a bustling village of small shops, artists, computer companies and the Village Grocery & Deli, a country store around which a town has grown. From there, the road can be followed to the junction of Vermont 100B for a trip toward Middlesex and the Middlesex Country Store, then continuing up U.S. Route 2 into Waterbury and turning on Vermont 100 to duck under Interstate 89 to Waterbury Center.

Back at the Roxbury Gap adventure, the route to the gap passes the East Warren Schoolhouse Market, a natural foods shop where Linda Faillace fought the U.S. Department of Agriculture during the mad sheep scare. Up the hill the pavement ends, but at the top is a scene of the entire ski area—just "the Valley" to local residents. At the bottom of the hill is tiny Roxbury, home of both equestrian and tennis camp Teela-Wooket and the Roxbury Country Store. Like many Vermont towns, Roxbury once supported three general stores, but by the 1980s all but one had vanished. The town, whose now-hidden quarry once provided *verde antique* marble to buildings across the United States, today is inhabited largely by loggers, farmers, artists, independent businesspeople and teachers—though some may remember it from a scene in Jack Nicholson's *Wolf*.

From the Roxbury Store north on Vermont 12A, the road joins Vermont 12 and onward through Northfield Falls to the Falls General Store at the corner of Cox Brook Road, the only place in the United States where three covered bridges can be seen at one time; the author lives between two of them. The next stop is Montpelier, where the Country Store unfortunately burned and was never reopened in downtown; it was a fine example of a small urban general store, not unlike F.H. Gillingham's in Woodstock. Route 2 goes east out of town.

The adventurous and timid meet in Waterbury Center, with a stop for snacks at the Center General Store before going on to the tourist mecca of Stowe; alas, the marvelous Moscow Store closed a few months before this writing. Once in town, it is easy to be blinded by Stowe's faux country stores along the Mountain Road (Vermont 108) to the west, so quickly find Shaw's General Store on Main Street. This 1895-era store carries dry goods and clothing, but is filled with mementos and photographs of the "real" Stowe that preceded the ski boom in the 1930s.

Following Vermont 100 north, the terrain changes into the rangy hills that border the Northeast Kingdom, and a turn south at Morrisville leads to Elmore State Park, Lake Elmore and the Elmore Store. Run by Kathy and Warren Miller (who is also a state representative), it is frequented by locals as well as Vermont's congressional delegation. The store, complete with post office, retains its lakeside character of utility and frugality, and is a perfect jumping-off point for a hike to the state park fire tower.

Backtracking along the road to Vermont 100 in summer, the traveler comes to Eden, the Eden General Store and campgrounds in Eden Mills along Lake Eden. True to its name, it is a pastoral setting ideal for a night's rest. If excitement is on the schedule, however, the route is not to Eden, but rather up Vermont 12 to Vermont 100 to Vermont 15 ("Grand Army of the Republic Highway") to the Hyde Park Village Market, up to Johnson with its arts-oriented state college and roadside restaurants, across to Jeffersonville and Hanley's General Store, through Cambridge and its General Store (more in Tour 8), across Vermont 104 to Fairfax and Minor's Country Store and eventually (via Vermont 128) into glittering Burlington for the night.

TOUR 5.

THE GREEN SCENE

Fair Haven to Bellows Falls
(1–2 days, 140 miles)

New York State—Fair Haven, Vermont—Hydeville—
Castleton—East Poultney—Pawlet—Danby—Peru—
Jamaica—Wardsboro—Newfane—Grafton—Chester—
Saxtons River—Bellows Falls

On entering Vermont via Fair Haven, take Vermont 4A to
Hydeville and Castleton, Vermont 30 and 140 to East Poultney,
back to Vermont 30 to Pawlet and the Danby-Pawlet Road and
U.S. Route 7 to Danby (Hydeville, Castleton, East Poultney,
Pawlet and Danby are described in Tour 1). From there head
down U.S. Route 7 through East Dorset to Manchester, grabbing
a left onto Vermont 11 east and heading up the mountain.

When coming through Peru, it is tempting to stay on
the main road, with its southward mountain vistas on the

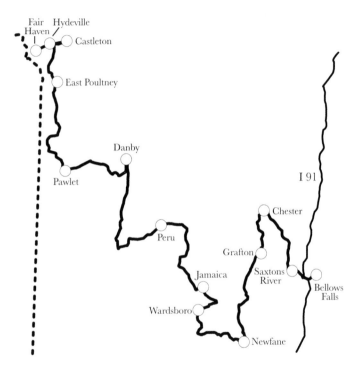

way past the Bromley Mountain Ski Area. Don't. Take the turnoff to Peru's center, which is the short old road that jogs off left and parallel to the highway. Go through the tiny front door to visit J.J. Hapgood's, which has the flavor and feel of a truly old store, with Sam Johnson and his family doing their home and store work together in the same rooms, with wood stove and pizza oven, old glass display case, cats, dogs and children. Have some pizza.

From Peru it is a long loop on Vermont 11 eastward to Vermont 30 to Jamaica Country Market and Noe Place, both in the tropically eponymous town, side-tripping to the Wardsboro Country Store on Vermont 100 south, backtracking to the tiny Harmonyville Store east on Vermont 30 and ultimately arriving at the Newfane Market.

Newfane Market was established in 1822 in the Windham County seat, the wooden building burning to the ground and being rebuilt in 1890. It is architectural motley: its porch was removed in 1940 and a new front was added in 1971, and striped awnings shade the windows in summer. Today the market emphasizes natural juices, vitamin water, beer and wine; Vermont products such as syrup, salsa and candy; and organic industrial hemp products including shampoo, soap and clothing. Stocking the traditional country store goods, the Newfane Market is heated solely by its wood stove, and features artist Johnny Swing's unusual metal chairs. Locals gather to talk, eat fresh baked goods and lean on the historical cabinetry.

LAZY DAYS IN THE HILLS

Massachusetts to Canada through the Green Mountains
(2–3 days, 275–300 miles)

Bernardston, Massachusetts—Guilford, Vermont—Putney—
Newfane—Saxtons River—Chester—Grafton—South
Woodstock—Woodstock
Scenic Route 1: Bridgewater Corners—Pittsfield
Scenic Route 2: Barnard
Meet at Bethel—Randolph Center—Snowsville—Barre—
North Montpelier—Adamant—Plainfield—Marshfield—
Cabot—West Danville—Greensboro—Glover—Orleans—
Evansville—West Charleston—Derby Line—Canada

Grab the map; this route twists and turns. Take U.S.
Route 5 to Guilford and Putney, Vermont 30 to Newfane
and then onto Vermont 121 to Saxtons River; 121, 103
and 11 to Chester; Vermont 11, 35 and 121 to Grafton.

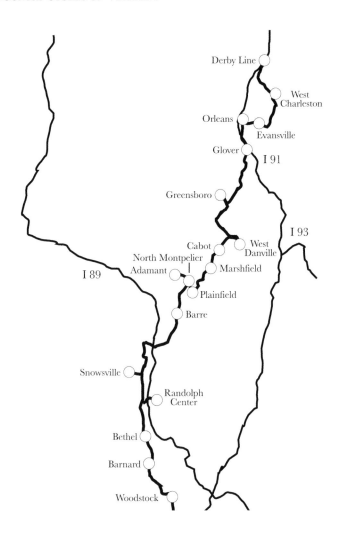

Derby Line

West
Charleston

Orleans

Evansville

Glover

I 91

Greensboro

I 93

Cabot

West
Danville

North Montpelier

Marshfield

Adamant

I 89

Plainfield

Barre

Snowsville

Randolph
Center

Bethel

Barnard

Woodstock

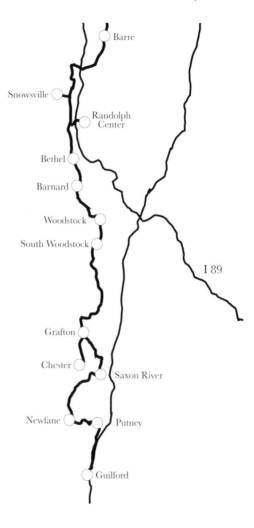

Barre

Snowsville

Randolph
Center

Bethel

Barnard

Woodstock

South Woodstock

I 89

Grafton

Chester

Saxon River

Newfane

Putney

Guilford

(Guilford, Putney, Saxtons River, Chester and Grafton are described in Tour 2, and Newfane is described in Tour 5.) Then Vermont 11, 103, 10 and 106 to South Woodstock.

You are now in horse country. The Green Mountain Horse Association is on the right as you head for the South Woodstock Country Store after a day of two-phase rides, hunter/jumper shows, cross-country, dressage and special events. A handsome brick building with classic shutters and a comfortable front porch, the store includes a fine bakery and makes legendary sandwiches—as well as keeping a full stock of every country store item you might expect. Especially in summer, the South Woodstock Country Store is crowded and conversational, so visiting on the porch is welcome.

Vermont 106 leads directly to the green in Woodstock, where a dogleg right and left arrives on Elm Street (Vermont 12) and F.H. Gillingham & Sons, a modest brick storefront in a downtown block.

The discontinuity of ownership of many country stores contrasts with F.H. Gillingham's in Woodstock, a fourth-generation business that has grown and changed with the town. The store, located downtown just off today's main street—and where the traffic used to flow to and through from the farms and towns to the north—was originally the small part of a front room, acquired from Mr. Hatch in the 1860s. F.H. Gillingham worked at the store after school, graduated from high school, formed a partnership and bought out Mr. Hatch. The store as it looks today was opened by Gillingham in 1886.

Gillingham's was not the typical little country store on a crossroads. Townspeople used to call their village the "City of Woodstock," and in the center of the "city" was F.H. Gillingham's, where farmers,

The staff of F.H. Gillingham's poses outside the store in the late nineteenth century. The "bug death" chemicals in the display window have been replaced by wines in 2008. *Courtesy Frank Billings, Woodstock.*

tradespeople, lawyers, doctors, teachers, blacksmiths and officials would congregate and exchange news while they lingered before the wood stove and picked up their mail at the post office inside.

The Woodstock Railroad spur went to central Woodstock, so perishable products could be brought from Boston and other production centers downcountry—at least until Clarence Birdseye, a friend of the family, helped the store become one of the country's first frozen food outlets. Old nail bins from mid-nineteenth century show years of wear, a reminder that Woodstock was once a farming community, with supplies and tools for sheep and dairy farms.

Jireh Billings, F.H. Gillingham's great-grandson, says, "As the town has grown up, so has Gillingham's. We started out being a farming community," providing fencing and the construction needs of the community, but now "we have a healthy second-home market," having followed the shift to tourism. Changes also took place inside the family; in 1945, Jireh's grandfather bought out his brother; in the early 1970s, his own parents began managing the store.

From its modest brick storefront, the store rambles back and back. Each room was added by a different family member with different interests. Copper torches sit next to hydroponic growing systems. Hardware evolved to sports equipment, and then from skiing's days of gut and wood to aircraft aluminum.

"The country store was the beginning of the department store era," Jireh explains. In addition to its historical dry goods, hardware and supplies, the store also stocked abundant housewares, wine, cheese, produce and specialty foods. Its fixtures date back to the mid-nineteenth century, and the large attic storage keeps hundred-year-old tools in ready-to-use condition. The original counters are still in place today—the worn surfaces belying the full networked computer system in the upstairs offices that keeps track of sales and inventory.

The building, now on the National Register of Historic Places, was built to specification in 1810 by local builder Titus Hutchison, with an office on one side and a store on the other side. Initially four stories, it was cut to a flat-roof, three-story building in 1936, and underwent major renovations, including a new art deco façade that was removed in the 1970s when Gillingham's was restored. The oldest building on Elm Street and the longest surviving in the center of town, it saw older buildings burn to the ground.

Through its lifetime, Gillingham's changed its practices as well. In the early nineteenth century, the store operated on cash as well as the barter system, and rare barter records survive from 1832. Shifting once again with the times, Gillingham's delivered groceries in the 1880s. In the late twentieth century, they began a mail-order company and established an Internet presence.

Gillingham's focuses on Vermont products, buying from small producers goods such as coffee, dessert sauces, pickles, mustards, condiments, honey, jams and jellies, maple syrup, wooden spoons, cutting boards and pottery. According to Billings, the store has a European flair—and an affluent clientele, meaning it also stocks expensive items and a diversity of products made outside New England to help the store's merchandising…and survival.

Such merchandising is not new; Jireh's grandfather was an expert. A customer had come into Gillingham's having eaten his first canned rattlesnake meat, effusively describing its succulence in detail, suggesting in his enthusiasm that it was something the store might order for him. The storekeeper listened, and when the story was over, he plucked a can off the shelf directly behind him and set it solidly on the counter, saying, "And here it is!"

F.H. Gillingham's in Woodstock looks little different than it did 150 years ago, except that wines are a new commodity in Vermont. *Courtesy Frank Billings, Woodstock.*

Gillingham's continues to anticipate trends. Twenty years ago, they began to enlarge the wine collection until it now makes up an entire room of wooden boxes stacked and opened in European fashion as locals and tourists alike see their changing tastes reflected in the stock. Gillingham's also has a philosophy of durability; Billings says, "We want things that are going to last and not end up in the landfill in a day or two," including steel and copper.

Billings repeats two comments often made by country store owners. The first is that the average

> country or general store's mix of products is greater than that of a big box store, and the second is repeated by voice, in paint and even in needlepoint: "If we don't have it, you don't need it."

There are two directions out of Woodstock, both worthwhile. One is the long loop west along U.S. Route 4 (just around the corner from Gillingham's) toward the Bridgewater Corners Country Store.

The store's convoluted history is typical and marvelous. It was first built by Ebenezer Clement in the mid-1840s, and successively became Walker & Babcock, Babcock & Wood, Wood & Mitchell and Babcock & Mitchell. Charles Babcock took the store alone in 1872, and his nephew Volney became postmaster. Then, according to the *Vermont Standard* of September 19, 1889, "The store of C. & V.C. Babcock at the Corners was entered early Wednesday AM. The safe blown open, money and books taken and fire set to the building. By 5:30 AM there was not a beam or sill left." In three weeks, lumber was being sawed, and the store reopened on the original foundation on January 16. Volney sold the store to H.G. Vaughan in 1896. It was Vaughan's Store until 1945, then Royal Fraser's until 1959, then Crockwell's, then just "the Corner Store" in 1972 under P. Ellis and M. O'Neil.

It became the Junction Store in 1976, the Junction Country Store until 1996 and finally the Bridgewater Corners Country Store under the ownership of Bob and Pat Hammond.

From Bridgewater Corners the route continues west on U.S. Route 4 until it joins Vermont 100 heading north toward Pittsfield (described in Tour 4) and onward at the fork via Vermont 107 to Bethel.

The other direction out of Woodstock is north on Vermont 12 to Barnard General Store on the banks of Silver Lake. The Barnard Store was established in 1832 and, with architectural alterations, stands as one of the longest-running general stores in the state. Its 1950s-era soda fountain is still in use, and its old wooden cabinets give the store a true vintage feel. During the summer months, Silver Lake is a popular swimming and boating spot, with a small dam over which North Road travels. From Barnard, either left on Vermont 12 or straight on the North Road will lead to Bethel; the author always takes the North Road.

Bethel is an old mill town whose Richardson's Store closed a decade ago when the children—as did those after the Civil War—moved on to a different life. The town has stately homes, brick buildings and the abandoned rail station that the Amtrak "Vermonter" passes twice each day.

Continuing out of town on Vermont 12 winds through a fertile valley, arriving in Randolph and its recently reopened rail station, onward to Vermont 66 that crosses Interstate 89 and arrives at Floyd's Store on the crossroads of Randolph Center.

Randolph Center is one of the surviving hill villages with homes and churches, built when the sun and warmth of the mountainside was the best way to prosper and remain healthy. Today the village is intact (and on the National Register of Historic Places) and is also the site of Vermont Technical College, the state's premier educational institution for high technology. Sitting at the crossroads with Williamstown to the north, Royalton to the south and Chelsea to the east, Floyd's General Store in Randolph Center is the perfect model for an old country store. It opened in 1843 with grain, hardware, feed and dry goods. Sleighs and buggies were manufactured there, and coffins were built and fitted upstairs. Later in the century, for reasons no one seems to recall, the store was lifted up and rolled on logs to its present site.

West Randolph was the valley town, growing up and prospering with the arrival of the Vermont Central Railroad, whose route took it toward Northfield to serve its owner and his hometown rather than through the more accommodating geography east of the hills. Despite the exodus into the valley, the road through the Center still remained the traveled route in winter, where snowfall averaged 110 inches and the road was kept packed hard by teams of horses

The original general store in Randolph Center was on the west side of the road. Late in the nineteenth century it was rolled across the street to the present site of Floyd's Store. *Courtesy Miriam Herwig, Randolph.*

and granite rollers. An area with surviving sheep farming, the remnants of Randolph Center's slate mining—with deposits that ran up through Slab City and beyond—are visible in the slate fence posts and directional markers.

The Center was also the home of Justin Morgan, who preached in the local church. The genetic errors that created the hardy Morgan horse named Figure were preserved by the music teacher and pioneering composer whose mysterious harmonies are still performed today in the Green Mountains.

The Morgan horse is Vermont's state animal, a strong breed with a stable personality well suited to the cool climate and long winters. Justin Morgan is buried in the cemetery by the road, and his original homestead is down the slope on Fish Hill Road.

Al and Jan Floyd bought the old store in town in 1963. Al recalls sliding from the store to the village as a child on his travois, before Interstate 89 was sliced through and made sled travel dangerous. They would get all the way down Slack Hill and hitch the travois to the nearest car to tow them back up. Today, snowmobiles ply the trail behind the store, which is otherwise a "summer road"—closed and, save for the snowmobile trails, invisible in winter. In summer, the nearby campground is filled with travelers heading for swimming and fishing, with hunting and foliage touring in autumn.

The effect of the interstates on so many Vermont general and country stores was to shade them from visibility to all but the adventurous tourist. But that did not bother Al and Jan, who made an effort *not* to change their approach to storekeeping. There are no computers in Floyd's, no inventory management system—just a mechanical cash register. There is no video rental, no lottery machine, no ATM. No credit cards are accepted; cash is welcome, along with a local check. Older customers still "run a slip."

Traffic going by on the interstate echoes up the hill, but Floyd's mostly takes care of their 90 percent local business, including people who have moved in from downcountry, building new homes on the rejuvenated hillsides. Their owners head home from work in other towns, and stop at Floyd's. And those immigrants brought with them tastes that have

Ice tongs, maple syrup, deli meats and cheeses, a wine bin and a barrel of onions share the view from the sitting area at Floyd's Store in Randolph Center.

changed—taste for fine wines, prepared and frozen foods, convenience foods, local salad dressings and artisan cheeses from nearby farms. Al and Jan make a point of stocking what is needed.

All of their changes also appeal to visitors, and Jan Floyd's resourcefulness appeals to everyone. Some come to Floyd's to sit and visit—inside, where table and chairs with magazines, books and games are found in winter, or outside, where a comfortable bench faces the green hillsides and western sun. If folks need help, Jan will pitch in. If something needs replacement, she says, "I can run home and get it, or help them fix it."

For most people, Floyd's is a quiet place. People run into neighbors on a summer evening, and older customers tell their stories. "They have all the time in the world, no hurry, so they do well here," she reflects, smiling as her black lab appears. "Holly is the real owner of the store, the general manager."

Back down the hill and right onto Vermont 12 northward curves through an agricultural valley where a lone old elm still leafs out every year. The speed limit drops before a tight dogleg, and that's Snowsville. Snowsville is not on the map, which lists it as East Braintree, but the Snowsville General Store is on the right. It is packed full—newspapers, food, magazines, snacks, syrup—but more than anything, it is a hunters' store. Heated by a wood stove where hunters warm up in the autumn season, Snowsville General sells hunting supplies, clothing, hunting and fishing licenses, rifles, shotguns, bows, turkey calls, fishing gear and worms, hats and gloves, camping goods, sunglasses, gun cleaning equipment, black powder and muzzleloading supplies and ammunition. Snowsville is a game reporting station, a service that some country stores dropped and to their surprise found it caused a downturn in customers. Vermont, despite the anti-hunting environmentalists who help keep the land clean and livable, remains a hunting culture. Snowsville reveals its depth.

Several miles north on Vermont 12, the road from Snowsville twists through the lush Brookfield Gulf, soon passing Vermont 65 on the right, into Allis State Park and farther onward across the Floating Bridge to East Brookfield. The pontoon bridge has been in place for a century, and drivers of low-slung cars might question the unpaved highway and the several inches of water that rise up to meet each crossing vehicle; the nervous traveler might continue into South Northfield and take the paved Vermont 64. Otherwise, after the floating bridge, a left turn onto Vermont 14 will lead to Williamstown, South Barre and into Barre and Dente's Market (described in the "Quarries" section).

Vermont 14 continues northward from Dente's until it arrives at U.S. Route 2, where the C.P. Dudley Store has been located since 1888. A typical crossroads general store in many ways, it also serves a complex community of visitors, students, loggers, doctors, farmers, lawyers, construction workers and teachers. With a two-story front porch, add-on buildings and gas pumps, Dudley's is a motley, but inside it is warm and friendly.

Get out the map to find Adamant. From Dudley's through North Montpelier and its Riverbend Store, there is a left onto Lightening Ridge Road to Adamant Road. Before granite was uncovered nearby, the town was called South Calais. Workers and families from Scotland and Canada congregated in the area when the quarries opened in 1880, filling boardinghouses and homes until more than one hundred men were working in the fourteen quarries. When the post office was established in 1893, the village had become Sodom, but the townspeople changed the name to Adamant in 1905, deciding it was "as hard but not as wicked."

The Adamant Co-Op looks little different from the house in which it was begun in 1935. With $200 worth of goods in a space rented from Minnie Horr, it was also a post office, and was not electrified until 1940. It sits on the same dirt crossroads, and it is still a post office.

Back down to Vermont 14 and eastward on U.S. Route 2 appear the towns of Plainfield (the Red Store) and

Marshfield. The Marshfield Village Store on the right, bright yellow and remembered for its feature role in the film *I Am the Cheese*, closed in the early spring of 2008. The tiny Cabot Village Store is next, followed by the Hastings Store in West Danville. At the junction of the Grand Army of the Republic, U.S. Route 2, the Lamoille Valley Railroad and Joe's Pond—just "the Pond" in local parlance—the Hastings Store has a long history of service to local residents and visitors alike.

The Hastings Store and post office is the last great building on the east side of the pond. The St. Johnsbury and Lamoille County railroad tracks are silent—they will soon be converted to a recreation trail—as are the late-night sounds of fiddlers and dancers in the vanished dance hall. Back in the day, according to Jane Hastings Larrabee, the store used to receive people's mail and phone messages and deliver them "up the pond," along with orders of groceries and dry goods. Visitors arriving for the summer would stay the season, with the only transportation to the scenic west side being by boat. So the Hastings family would deliver one day to one side of the pond, the next day to the other side.

The Hastings Store was built around 1853 as a stagecoach stop and inn, and served the train station near the Joe's Pond beach. The Hastings family purchased the store from Burt Wells in 1913, learning to heat the store with wood and clean, fill and light the kerosene lamps each day. Gristmills and sawmills also crowded the roadside, and Hastings used to have a soda fountain popular with millworkers. After World War II, coffee became the drink of choice, but before the war, it was the milkshake. One mill owner was temperamental and would often fire the whole crew, who then visited the store for milkshakes. About lunchtime the owner would come over for a milkshake himself…and hire them all back.

There was rumrunning during Prohibition in towns where roads and railroads came together. In the morning one might go across to the gas station to see the latest car with bullet holes in its back—but no one ever got caught in West Danville. Residents recall that the driver was a deaf woman who did not hear gunfire and never got rattled.

Directly across the road was a casket factory. "If anyone died, they'd have them measured up," says Jane. The church was built in 1893, and before the first funeral, one parishioner said he did not care for the minister and would kick the side out of the coffin when he died if this minister performed the funeral services. When the man eventually died, a new casket factory helper screwed down the coffin's top—but put nails in its bottom. As the casket was brought around the church, the bottom fell out and the late parishioner got his revenge.

Ice was important to every country store in the days before electricity and mechanical refrigeration—even though Hastings was electrified in 1925. Stores had to stock cold food in summer, have iced drinks and make ice cream. In cities, the iceman mysteriously delivered the blocks. But in the country? It was cut from frozen ponds and stored. Ice cutting on Joe's Pond was done at a rate of two hundred blocks per day. Hand tools were used, including eight-foot saws and heavy tongs to heave the ice onto an old truck rolled onto the pond. A hole was made in the ice with thick steel rod "chippers" with a claw at the bottom. A row was cut, pipes were run out to an inclined plane, the blocks were slid and dragged into the truck and the load was stacked in the icehouse.

January was the best month to cut, especially during the annual thaw when the ice was eighteen to twenty-four inches thick. According to Jane, who

Cutting the ice on Joe's Pond in West Danville. After sweeping the ice, the chipper and saws as long as eight feet were used to cut blocks. *Courtesy Jane Hastings Larrabee.*

was just a few years old at the time, "Everybody took a dip in the pond at some time during the ice cutting"—including seventy-eight-year-old Ed Houghton. Grandfather Gilbert Hastings worked on it along with Jane's father Ralph, with help from around town. Once the ice was cut and packed in the icehouse in layers of sawdust—the icehouse had blocks fifteen feet deep, the size of a barn—it would last to the end of August.

A finished block is being loaded onto the truck in 1950, after which it will be brought to the icehouse and stored in sawdust through August. *Courtesy Jane Hastings Larrabee.*

The meat case had to be filled with ice then, but is now used for storage. Before freezers and coolers, the ice helped make ice cream for the warm days. Jane's grandmother Jenny Hastings would cut meats, and grew her own garden with herbs and spices to make sausage; Jane still uses her mother Mabel's recipe, but no longer grows and grinds her own sage as her grandmother did.

Ice cutting came to an end in West Danville when Jane's father injured his back. Soon the village mills were gone, then one by one the casket factory, rake factory, shingle factory, regular sawmill and the granite-cutting shed.

Today, the store remains full of goods, still has the post office inside and serves to-go meals, groceries, freshly cut meats and home-baked pastries and breads. Snowmobilers drop in all winter from the VAST trails behind the store. Though the train stopped running in the 1980s and the area is becoming a park, the Hastings Store serves box lunches to the daily train tours.

Because it remains so much a farming community with small villages far from commercial centers, Vermont's Northeast Kingdom has country stores to serve them. Taking Vermont 15 north from West Danville through Walden and onto Vermont 16, the traveler arrives in Greensboro Bend. Once a small center, today it is hardly more than a left turn toward Greensboro itself.

On the banks of Caspian Lake, Greensboro is a Victorian vacation town. Its historical society has a photo taken from the hilltop showing a village with horse-drawn sleighs, and a later one with touring cars clustered at the local general stores. Today, those stores are conjoined as Willey's Store, with groceries, clothes, newspapers, syrup, maps, wine and even hanging wagon wheels adorned with leather straps of sleigh bells. A study in contrast, the store uses computerized checkout lanes with solid tops of local rock maple.

From Cemetery Ridge to Young Road, the route leads back to Vermont 16 and northward to Glover, a town given worldwide notoriety by the Bread & Puppet Theater, initiators of the "Cheap Art" philosophy and creators of the homely giant puppets that often appear at peace demonstrations. Though Bread & Puppet is frequently at odds with the town, Currier's Market is not. Jim Currier's store is the centerpiece of the community, not merely because it is the store (and post office) in which everyone gathers for goods from groceries to hardware to beer to fan belts to bait to plumbing, but also because it has one of the largest collections of stuffed animals, mounted antlers and heads and even wasps' nests in Vermont. From owls to deer to bears to panthers to foxes to pheasants and even the moose that guards the post office, the Currier's Market animals are everywhere in the store, staring down at patrons from walls and up at them from displays of beverages. Currier's may not appeal to some latter-day sensibilities, but it is a stunning visit on the road into the Kingdom.

From Glover it is a short ride from Vermont 16 to U.S. Route 5 through Orleans and its Northern Exposure Country Store to the Evansville Trading Post on Vermont 58.

The Evansville Trading Post exemplifies how stores may unexpectedly appear in underserved areas—exactly as they did in Vermont two hundred years ago. Leon E. Swett ran the Up-To-Date Grocery for thirty-five years in Orleans. Leon's business did well until World War II, but then he was pushed out by the first wave of competitive challenges—the supermarkets.

Leon left the grocery business and took up farming in the Brownington area with his son Ralph, now known as Chief Lone Cloud. But the future chief's childhood experiences informed his future. He became chairman of the Bicentennial Committee in 1975, writing a book on the history of Brownington. His involvement in the community led to the local church, which had been occupied by young people the locals called "the hippies." Ralph wrote to the Methodist bishop, offering $2,000 for the church; his offer was accepted and he began selling what he described as "junk, antiques and furniture. There's a lot of money in junk, you know."

Then the transformation into a country store began. Ralph built a two-car garage in the back. He "hitched an old barn to it" and built another garage and a henhouse. The store was growing piece by piece, and when the little store in Brownington center—the last in the area—"was slowly going out like all little stores do," the transformation began in earnest. Although he recognized there was more profit in furniture than groceries, Ralph responded to local requests and opened the Evansville Trading Post in 1977. In short order "it was going pretty damn good."

So came into being the only Native American country store in Vermont. Ralph was contacted by the old chief in Wilder, and in the early 1980s, the organization began for the first Vermont powwow. The gathering took place in 1992, after which Ralph—Chief Lone Cloud—helped establish an Abenaki museum and shop in Brownington. The chief believes in service and says, "The biggest thing is to help people get back to their heritage—family groups, education in schools, young people, work in prisons."

The Evansville Trading Post has a gift shop, new freezers and shelving and remodeled grocery with seafood and meats, along with the store's traditional stocks of hardware and animal feed. Like H.N. Williams in Dorset, Dan & Whit's in Norwich, Wayside in West Arlington and Currier's in Glover, if the chief doesn't have it, then you don't need it.

At Evansville Trading Post, the only Native American–owned country store in Vermont, handmade goods and art occupy an entire room.

The chief is concerned about his store. "Country stores are having a very hard time," he says. The winter of 2007 was slow, with customers bleeding to the big box stores that are having an impact throughout Vermont. Despite its long-standing hunting tradition, Evansville stopped selling guns: it costs more for the store to buy them than hunters pay in the box stores.

"It wasn't the biggest moneymaker," says the chief, "but we had $30,000 invested in it." He sold the lot with special deals and at gun auctions. "It used to be a good part of our business, but the last year or two it wasn't."

The gun room at the Evansville Trading Post in 2006, before economic pressures from big box stores emptied it a year later.

Chief Lone Cloud writes a local column about the store. Not long ago he wrote, "It was always pleasant to go to a small local store and receiving a big smile and 'Howdy do.' And when you were small, getting a sucker or other small candy, *free?* What a treat that was! And above all, adults would get a local newspaper, a cup of coffee and the time to visit with friends and neighbors, catching up on local news and gossip. It was a time of sharing and caring. It was such a great feeling and a wonderful way to start the day."

Leaving Evansville Trading Post eastward joins Vermont 5A north to Charleston and West Charleston into Derby Line (described in Tour 2) and into Canada for the night.

EAST/WEST TRAILBLAZING

Fair Haven to White River
(1 day, 120 miles)

New York State—Fair Haven, Vermont—Hydeville—Castleton—Mendon—Bridgewater Corners—Plymouth—Ludlow—Chester—Woodstock—Taftsville—White River Junction

Almost all the towns in this tour are found as part of other tours, but this unique venture finds its way across Vermont where "you can't get there from here." Follow Tour 4 to Mendon, and onward on U.S. Route 4 to Bridgewater Corners (Tour 6), onto Vermont 100A south toward Plymouth and its country store, with the Calvin Coolidge birthplace and homestead. Join Vermont 100 south toward Ludlow and follow deep into the mountain forest toward its two country stores along the old Green Mountain Turnpike

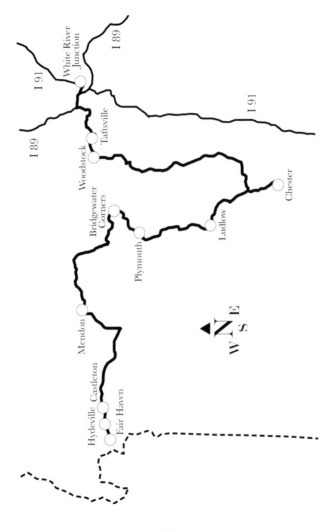

and beside the meandering Lake Rescue. Turn eastward on Vermont 103 past the turn to Cavendish (where exiled novelist Alexander Solzhenitsyn lived for seventeen years) and arriving in Chester (described in Tour 2).

The thirty miles to Woodstock turns east to Vermont 11, and onto Vermont 106 in Springfield through Downers, Felchville and South Woodstock and its country store into Woodstock (described in Tour 6) and east onto U.S. Route 4 to Taftsville.

The Taftsville Country Store is nestled in the scenic Ottauquechee River Valley, on U.S. Route 4 midway between Woodstock and Quechee. The store is the centerpiece of the Taftsville Historic District, which includes one of Vermont's oldest and longest covered bridges, a turn-of-the-century brick powerhouse, the stately Taft homes and a quiet residential hamlet of fewer than one hundred people.

The Taftsville store followed the arc of country stores throughout Vermont—initially built to provide for the community that grew up around it, and slowly shifting focus as the area changed from founders to millworkers to a drained population and then general tourism. In 1793, blacksmith Stephen Taft left Uxbridge, Massachusetts, and settled in what is now known as Taftsville. Three years later, his brother Daniel joined Stephen in Vermont, but they would wait until 1840 before the younger brother built the store under the name Daniel Taft & Sons. It was a Federal-style brick building sitting on what was the Woodstock-Windsor Turnpike. In 1855, however, the Tafts were gone and the "Brick Store Lot" was sold at auction for $450 to Carlos Hamilton of Hartford, who operated a Union Store until 1864. At some point the road shifted a hundred feet north as a free road, and then the store's history is blank until 1872—even though it remained open—when "Job" Marcy operated the store simply as Merchant and Grocer through 1895. From 1896 to 1918, W.H. and Betsy Brownell were entrepreneurs variously described as "makers of cider jelly, etc." (1896–99), "Groceries" (1900–01), "Merchants & Gen. Mdse. & Mfgrs." (1902–04) and "General Mdse. and Saw & Grist Mill" (1905–06). They also had a small machine and wood shop in the old carriage house and garage, and likely owned the sawmill across the river. The store was run from 1918 to 1922 by the Thompsons, who once more changed its merchandising, this time to an ice cream parlor called Butternut Lodge. The shop was shifted to Fred Kelly, who in 1922 established the

Attic, one of the first antique shops in the area. Four years later it was purchased by Charles Koller, who once again opened a general store. In 1940, he turned the business over to Harvey Dietrichs, continuing until it became Watson's Country Store in 1957 under the guidance of Harvey and Pearl Watson. It was transferred in 1982 to the Howes, who established the Taftsville Country Store & Gifts, and then shifted to Ron and Kathy King, owners and operators from 1987 to 1991, when current owner Charles Wilson purchased the Taftsville Country Store.

It has served 160 years, all but four as a country store. Yet once on a crossroads by the river, the Taftsville Store is no longer a central location with fast traffic passing it by. Wilson—who still lives upstairs—has expanded the mail-order business begun in 1957 with strong Internet visibility, and in the store with a new green built in 2005, Wilson emphasizes tourist items along with local cheeses, sodas, condiments, maple syrup and candy, honey and recordings, as well as Vermont Common Crackers, local soaps and postcards. For the fishing trade he offers night crawlers and worms. He has groceries such as sugar, flour, frozen goods, cigars and beer, and an expanding curated wine collection. The store maintains the post

The staff of the Taftsville Country Store. Many Vermont products, including a wide range of artisan cheeses, join the newspapers, goodies and souvenirs at the register.

office in the carriage house portion of the building, newly restored in the late 1990s. Though Wilson publicly (in the *New York Times*) fought the government for several years to keep the post office open and in the store with its full-time postmaster, he modestly says, "Think of old Cal Coolidge. We've made a cachet of boring."

The Taftsville store has old metal ceilings, brick chimneys and a working wood stove. Posters of local events cover the windows—work wanted, services offered. A tractor pulls up for lunch as Wilson relates how he fled Los Angeles and corporate life for Vermont. "I settled for a small business I could call my own," he says, eager to feel part of the community, stand behind a cash register and walk around the village in the evening. He calls the two dogs his "store managers."

Wilson saw his business move to one-third local in Vermont and New Hampshire, one-third tourist and one-third mail order. Wilson emphasizes Vermont products. "I'm a real stickler on that," he says. What can be produced in Vermont must be produced in Vermont, he believes, not made elsewhere with a Vermont P.O. box. His Vermont farm cheese is cut to order—sheep's milk, goat's milk, cow's milk, brie, camembert, asiago, fontina, gouda and blue. "No New York cheddar carried here," he laughs, now fiercely loyal to Vermont.

From Taftsville, the road continues east to U.S. Route 5, and northward to the railroad town of White River Junction.

TOUR 8.

ONWARD TO THE KINGDOM

Rutland to Derby Line
(2–3 days, 240–250 miles)

Follow Tour 4: New York—Fair Haven, Vermont—Hydeville—
Castleton—Rutland—Mendon—Pittsford—Leicester—
Ripton—Bristol—Jerusalem Corners
Scenic Route 1: Jericho Center—Cambridge—Hyde Park—
Wolcott
Scenic Route 2: Buel's Gore to Waitsfield—Duxbury—
Waterbury Center—Middlesex—East Montpelier
Meet at Woodbury
Then follow Tour 6 to Marshfield—Cabot—West Danville—
Greensboro—Glover—Orleans—Evansville—West
Charleston—Derby Line—Canada

The route to Pittsford is described in Tours 1 and 4—
Fair Haven via Vermont 4A to Hydesville and Castleton,

Derby Line
West Charleston
Orleans
Evansville
Glover
Cambridge
Hyde Park
Greensboro
Jericho Center
Wolcott
Woodbury
West Danville
Cabot
Marshfield
Jerusalem Corners
Bristol
I 89
I 91
Ripton
Leicester
Pittsford
Hydeville Castleton Mendon
Fair Haven Rutland

Derby Line
West Charleston
Orleans
Evansville
Glover
Greensboro
Woodbury
Waterbury Center
West Danville
Cabot
Duxbury
Middlesex
Marshfield
Buel's Gore
East Montpelier
Jerusalem Corners
Waitsfield
Bristol
I 89
I 91
Ripton
Leicester
Pittsford
Hydeville
Castleton
Mendon
Rutland
Fair Haven

there to U.S. Route 4 in Rutland, optionally to Mendon via U.S. Route 4 (or U.S. Route 7) from Rutland to Pittsford.

Northward from Pittsford passes through Brandon and arrives in Leicester. The crossroads store is gone in this village near Lake Dunmore, so a right turn to the lake is a welcome summer respite—especially if you want to say you've been to Satan's Kingdom, Vermont, a desolate cove at the south end of the lake. Continuing from Satan's Kingdom east on Vermont 73 and then north on Vermont 100, the trip includes Rochester and Hancock, and a left on Vermont 125 leads to Ripton (Rochester, Hancock and Ripton are described in Tour 4).

Turning north on Vermont 116 leads very scenically to Vermont 17 and Bristol, a brick strip town with elegant buildings such as Holly Hall, the town hall with ornate brick architecture and a unique bell tower. The Village Corner Store is packed with groceries, animal feed, newspapers and even a deli in its tiny space.

Continuing on Vermont 17 is a summer trip. The road is open in winter, but see the travel guide for more about winter driving in Vermont. On the right is the Jerusalem Corners Country Store, founded in 1969 and one of Vermont's newer country stores. Jerusalem Corners is a desolate spot in midwinter, but the vistas are stunning, including the spine of the Green Mountains that the road is about to skirt.

Outside Jerusalem Corners, Vermont 17 eventually begins to ascend across the Appalachian Gap into Fayston, but this tour option follows Gore Road through Hanksville, Huntington and Richmond. Heading straight at Richmond slides under Interstate 89 onto the Jericho Road and up Brown's Trace Road. Watch the bumps. You will soon be in Jericho Center and the oldest operating country store in Vermont.

Jericho Center was settled shortly after the French and Indian War, with its first meetinghouse built in 1794. Pliny Blackman was trading local goods for fabrics by traveling to Montréal, ultimately opening a store in Jericho Center in 1808. The store served mills—saw, grist and woolen—and the town grew to include several stores, a Congregational church and a library. The Burlington and Lamoille Railroad arrived in 1876; just up the road in Jericho nine years later, Wilson Bentley would take the first photograph of a single snowflake, and the Jericho Center store would shortly change hands to Eugene and Henry Jordan. After the town's other store burned, the Jordans enlarged their store and gave it the peculiar Victorian front it has today, including the only eight-sided window in a Vermont general store.

Henry Jordan died in 1911, and disaster struck in 1914 as nearly twelve inches of rain fell in one afternoon, washing out most of the town's bridges and roads. The store survived and helped the Center recover. Wayne Nealy became a partner in 1917, and purchased the store in 1922. It became Blackman's, then Newton's in 1958, Desso's General in 1965 and Jericho Center Market in 1995, and finally the Jericho Center Country Store under Linda and Doug St. Amour in 2002.

The Jericho Center country store as it looks today. Other than a few coats of paint and the gas pumps, it has looked unchanged since the late nineteenth century. *Jon St. Amour, Jericho Center.*

The Jericho Center store when it was Jordan Brothers in the early twentieth century. The store was built in 1808, and the façade changed some eight years later. *"Morton"; courtesy Jon St. Amour, Jericho Center.*

Jon St. Amour describes the current store: "We are a working post office, issue fire permits, hold town keys for the library, church and community center. Our store is full of amazing antiques, including eighty-year-old post office boxes, a one-hundred-year-old storefront 'Kellogg's Corn Flakes' sign and even a case of very old embalming fluid." The present store has groceries and newspapers, Vermont products, beer and wine, a deli, a well-used checkerboard, pies from the wood-fired oven and holiday turkeys and hams.

Corinne Wilder Thompson recalls, "There was this large heating grate and there was a table nearby. People would sit around the table, talk and play cards and checkers. Soldiers especially from down at the [Ethan Allen Firing] Range would come in and play checkers. I was in high school then. A Coke was nine cents. Candy bars were three cents, but you could get a quarter-pound candy bar for ten cents."

Continuing north out of Jericho Center joins Vermont 15 north out of Underhill Flats to Cambridge and the Village Market, a grocery store with an unbroken history back to the 1850s. The original Willy Brothers Store became the Cambridge Community Lockers, where residents would rent refrigerator and freezer space to store their food. The lockers are gone now, removed in the 1950s. At the end of the twentieth century, the store—a wood structure with a second-story porch—expanded without destroying its character.

Vermont 15 backtracks a short distance west through Jeffersonville to Hyde Park and its Village Market, and across to the Wolcott Store. A scenic ride south after a turn onto Vermont 14 at Hardwick leads south through Woodbury, where its store reopened to community celebration.

The other direction out of Jerusalem Corners is toward Buel's Gore, the uninhabited top of the Appalachian Gap along Vermont 17 east with its grand western vistas, arriving in Waitsfield and north on Vermont 100 through Duxbury—town of "summer farmer, winter woodsman"—and its country store. A trip north through Waterbury will tuck under Interstate 89 to Waterbury Center, or south on U.S. Route 2 will pass through Montpelier and up to East Montpelier and the C.P. Dudley Store (see Tour 6), joining Vermont 14 north onward to Woodbury.

From Woodbury, Tour 6 takes over from Marshfield to Derby Line.

ON THE MILITARY ROAD

Wells River to Canada via the Bayley-Hazen Military Road
(1–2 days, 135 miles)

Wells River—Boltonville—Ryegate Corner—Mosquitoville—
South Peacham—Peacham—west of Ewells Mills—West
Danville—Cabot Plains—South Walden—Taylor Bridge—
Dows Crossing—Tolmans Corner—Campbells Corner—
east of East Craftsbury—west of Albany—Lowell—Hazen's
Notch (end)—Westfield—Troy—North Troy—Canada

Tour 9 is a special ride, especially conducive to summer days
on a motorcycle. The Bayley-Hazen Road is often obscured
and ends in trails, and the country stores along the route
are quietly vanishing. Grab a good map or a GPS unit,
and as you pass through these villages, the metal, concrete
and stone markers will outline the old Revolutionary road.
Tumbledown stone fences, rock foundations and patches of

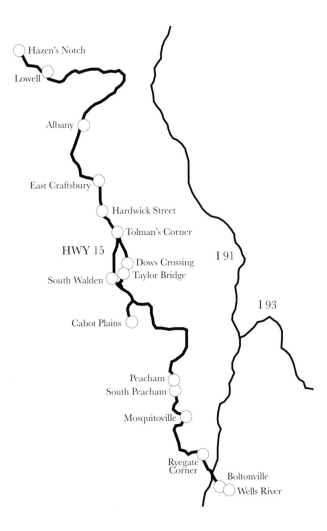

Hazen's Notch

Lowell

Albany

East Craftsbury

Hardwick Street

Tolman's Corner

HWY 15

Dows Crossing

Taylor Bridge

South Walden

Cabot Plains

I 91

I 93

Peacham

South Peacham

Mosquitoville

Ryegate Corner

Boltonville

Wells River

day lilies will be the only reminders of the Revolutionary Patriots and the Northeast Kingdom pioneers with their homes and businesses.

1. Start at **Wells River**
2. Central Street/U.S. 302→ Bible Hill Road→ Ryegate Corner-Boltonville Road (South Bayley-Hazen Road)→ **Ryegate Corner**
3. Witherspoon Road→ Hall Road→ Mosquitoville Road→ **Mosquitoville**
4. Mosquitoville Road→ Schoolhouse Road→ Gadley Hill Road→ Groton Road→ Peacham-Groton Road→ **South Peacham**
5. Bayley-Hazen Road→ **Peacham**
6a. *Summer*: Continue and take fork to Joe's Pond Road passing west of **Ewells Mills**
6b. *Summer*: Trail goes west; continue on Paradise Road→ U.S. Route 2→ **West Danville**→ Cabot Plains Road→ **Cabot Plains**
6c. *Winter*: Bayley-Hazen Road→ Peacham-Danville Road→ Danville, U.S. Route 2→ Vermont 15→ Bayley-Hazen Road→ Cabot-Plains Road→ **Cabot Plains**
7. Road ends at Cabot Plains; turn around and take Bayley Hazen Road→ Vermont 215→ Vermont 15→ east of **South Walden**
8. Cross Vermont 15 (Grand Army of the Republic Road)→ Bayley-Hazen Road→ **Taylor Bridge**

9. Continue on Bayley-Hazen Road→ **Dows Crossing**

10. Continue on Bayley-Hazen Road→ **Tolmans Corner**

11. Trail goes west; take Ward Hill Road→ Main Street→ Church Street→ Hardwick Street to **Hardwick Street** (a street and a place)

12. Continue on Hardwick Street→ Lake Shore Road→ Lakeview Road→ **Campbells Corner**

13. Trail now crosses various roads; take Lakeview Road→ Lake Shore Road→ Richardson Road→ Whetstone Brook Road→ East Craftsbury Road→ Ketchum Hill Road→ **East Craftsbury**

14. Trail is east; take Ketchum Hill Road→ Young Road→ Auld Lang Syne Road→ North Craftsbury Road through Craftsbury Common, where the trail goes through mountains; take North Craftsbury Road→ Vermont 14 toward **Albany**

15. There is no direct route to Lowell, as all the mountain roads are closed; take Vermont 14→ Irasburg→ Vermont 58→ **Lowell**

16. Vermont 58→ **Hazen's Notch.** This is the end of the original Bayley-Hazen Military Road

17. You can hike the Long Trail to Canada, or drive back to Lowell and take Route 100 north→ **Westfield**

18. Route 100→ **Troy**

19. Vermont 101→ Vermont 105→ **North Troy**→ **Canada** Provincial 243

The Country and General Stores and Markets of Vermont

Not much of an address? Go into town and ask—and call before you go! Sadly, country stores may disappear. In the past five years, eighteen stores have closed and seven became other businesses. (*denotes members of the Vermont Alliance of Independent Country Stores)(All stores are area code 802)*

1836 Country Store, West Main Street, Wilmington 05363, 464-5102

A&B Beverage, 193 U.S. Route 2, Grand Isle 05458, 372-4531

*Adamant Co-Op, 1313 Haggett Road, Adamant 05640, 223-5760

Addison Four Corners Store, 4934 Vermont Route 22A, Vergennes 05491, 759-2332

Albany General Store, 842 Main Street, Albany 05820, 755-6222

Aldrich's General Store, 196 Vermont Route 5A, West Burke 05871, 467-3367

Alley's Market, South Ryegate 05069, 584-4416

Almost Home Market, 28 North Street, Bristol 05443

Al's Country Store, 3699 Woodstock Road, White River Junction 05001, 295-7563

B&B Cash Market, West Fairlee 05083, 333-9350

B&D Supermarket, 67 Main Street, North Troy 05859, 988-2545

Bailey's & Burke, East Burke 05832, 626-9250

Baker's Store, 7788 Vermont Route 113, Thetford 05074, 333-9350

Bakersfield General Store, Bakersfield 05441, 827-3738

Bakersfield Village Market, 31 Main Street, Bakersfield 05441, 827-6140

*Barnard General Store, Barnard 05031, 234-9688

Barnet Village Store, Church Street, Barnet 05821, 633-2302

Barnie's Market, 1120 Willson Road, North Concord 05858, 695-8133

Barton Village Corner Store, 155 Main Street, Barton 05822, 525-1243

Bay Store, St. Albans Bay 05481, 524-4227

Beaudry's Store, 2175 Main Road, Huntington 05642, 434-2564

Bedard Cash Market, 137 Library Avenue, Rutland 05701, 747-6910

Bellomo's Market, 31 Forest Street, Rutland 05701, 775-1632

Belmont General Store, 2400 Belmont Road, Belmont 05730, 259-2292

Bennett's Cavendish General Store, 1990 Main, Cavendish 05142, 226-7751

Benson Village Store, 774 Lake Road, Benson 05731, 537-2041

Bill's Country Store, U.S. Route 4, Killington 05751, 773-9313

*Bliss Village Store, Bradford 05033, 222-4617

*Bridgewater Corners Country Store, U.S. Route 4, Bridgewater Corners 05035, 672-6241

Bristol Country Store, 3191 South Vermont Route 116, Bristol 05443, 453-4164

Bromley Market, 376 Vermont Route 11, Peru 05152, 824-4444

Brookfield Valley Store, 6059 Vermont Route 14, Brookfield 05036, 276-3200

Brookside Country Store, Vermont Route 14, Barre 05641, 476-5560

Brownsville General Store, 871 Vermont Route 44, Windsor 05089, 484-7450

Budzyn's Country Store, Vermont Route 12A, Randolph 05060, 728-9901

Burnett's Country Store, Vergennes 05491, 475-2431

*Buxton's Store, 499 Main Street, Orwell 05760, 948-2112

Byam's Quick Stop, 4573 Lake Road, Franklin 05457, 933-4100

Cabot Village Store, 3109 Main Street, Cabot 05647, 563-2438

Calais General Store, 4520 Vermont Route 14, East Calais 05650, 456-8861

Cambridge General Store, Vermont Route 15, Cambridge 05444, 644-8861

*Cambridge Village Market, 113 South Main Street, Cambridge 05444, 644-2272

*Castleton Village Store, Main Street, Castleton 05735, 468-2213

Center General Store, 2026 Blush Hill Road, Waterbury Center 05677, 244-7500

Center Market, 3897 Ethan Allen Highway, Saint Albans 05478, 524-3240

Central Market, 50 Summer Street, Barre 05641, 476-4888

Central Market, Bethel 05032, 234-9010

Chapman's General Store, U.S. Route 5, Fairlee 05045, 333-9709

Charlie's General Store, U.S. Route 7, Wallingford 05773, 446-2274

Chick's Market, 60 Hickok Street, Winooski 05404, 655-0112

Chippenhook General Store, 13 Old Mill Road, Arlington 05250, 375-8389

Christy's Market, Vermont Route 100, West Dover 05356, 464-3882

Cindee's Country Store, U.S. Route 5, St. Johnsbury 05819, 748-7144

Clarendon Springs General Store, Clarendon Springs Road, North Clarendon 05759, 438-5153

Clute's Lake Eden Country Store, 4131 Vermont Route 100, Eden Mills 05653, 635-2692

*Coburn's General Store, South Strafford 05070, 765-4421

Cole's Market, 52 Main Street, Orleans 05860, 754-6015

Cone's Point Market, Vermont Route 30, Wells 05774, 287-9925

C.P. Dudley Store, 2915 U.S. Route 2, East Montpelier 05651, 223-2792

Craftsbury Country Store, 25 South Craftsbury Road, Craftsbury 05826, 586-2811

Crossroads Trading Post, 2805 Cookeville Road, Corinth 05039, 439-6060

Crosstown General Store, 3721 Country Road, Montpelier 05602, 485-4989

Crystal Beach Market, Vermont Route 30, Bomoseen 05732, 273-2666

Cullinan's Store, Arlington 05250, 375-6466

*Currier's Quality Market, 1 Main Street, Glover 05839, 525-8822

D&R General Store, Vermont Route 121, Cambridgeport 05141, 869-2372

Dan & Sheila's Country Store, 21 Church Street, Waterville 05492, 644-6555

*Dan & Whit's General Store, Main Street, Norwich 05055, 649-1602

*Danby Four Corners Store, 5 Danby Pawlet Road, Danby 05739, 293-5316

*Debanville's General Store, 47 Vermont Route 105, Guildhall 05905, 962-3311

*Dente's Market, 406 North Main Street, Barre 05641, 476-3764

Derby Village Store, 483 Main Street, Derby 05829, 766-2215

Derek's Country Store, Lower Cabot Road, Marshfield 05658, 563-2865

Desourcie's Market, Highgate Center 05459, 868-4409

Diamond Hill Store, 23 Hill Street, Danville 05828, 684-9797

Dick & Pam's Market, 2813 Vermont Route 105, East Berkshire 05447, 933-2153

Dick Mazza's General Store, 777 West Lakeshore Drive, Colchester 05446, 862-4065

Doris's Corner Store, 22 River Road, Lemington 05903, 266-3526

Dorset Union Store (formerly Peltier's), 31 Church Street, Dorset 05251, 867-4400

Dutchie's Grocer, 27 Railroad Street, West Pawlet 05755, 645-0069

Duxbury Country Store, 2542 Vermont Route 100, Waterbury 05676, 244-7546

East Calais General Store, 4520 Vermont Route 14, East
Calais 05648, 456-8861

East Charleston Country Store, East Charleston 05833, 723-
4303

East Clarendon General Store, Vermont Route 103, North
Clarendon 05759, 786-0948

East Corinth General Store, 8392 Vermont Route 25, East
Corinth 05040, 439-5525

*East Poultney General Store, South Main Street, East
Poultney 05741, 287-4042

East Randolph Country Store, East Randolph 05041,
728-5750

Eden General Store, Eden 05652, 635-7534

Elmore Store, 1208 Vermont Route 12, Lake Elmore 05657,
888-2296

*Evansville Trading Post, 645 Evansville Road, Brownington
05860, 754-6305

Falls General Store, 7 Cox Brook Road, Northfield 05663,
485-8044

*F.H. Gillingham & Sons, 16 Elm Street, Woodstock 05091,
457-2100

Flanders Market, 357 Vermont Route 110, Chelsea 05038,
685-3085

Fletcher General Store, 110 School Road, Cambridge
05444, 849-6292

*Floyd's Store, Randolph Center 05061, 728-5333

Forest Country Store, State Forest Boulder, Groton 05046, 584-4899

Franklin General Store, 5243 Main Street, Franklin 05457, 285-2033

G&L General Store, 2813 Vermont Route 22A, Benson 05731, 537-4041

The General Store, 4520 Vermont Route 14, East Calais 05650, 456-8861

Gihon River Store, 4495 Vermont Route 100C, Johnson 05656, 635-1767

Grafton Grocery Market, Grafton 05146, 843-1196

Granby General Store, 8910 Granby Road 05840, 328-2630

Granger Street Market, 172 Granger Street, Rutland 05701, 773-9898

*Graniteville General Store, Graniteville 05654, 476-5088

Grant's Village Store, 8 East Street, Middletown Springs, 05757, 235-2251

Guilford Country Store, 475 Coolidge Highway, Brattleboro 05301, 254-9898

Hall's Market, Mill Street, Hardwick 05843, 472-6677

Hanley's General Store, Vermont Route 15, Jeffersonville 05464, 644-8881

Harborside Harvest Market, North Hero 05474, 372-4443

*Harbor View General Store, Hydeville 05750, 265-8884

Harmonyville Store, Vermont Route 30, Townshend 05353, 365-9417

Hasgas General Store, 69 Vt. Rt. 30, Dorset 05251, 362-4250

*Hastings Store, West Danville 05873, 684-3398

Henry's Market, 831 Main Street, Bennington 05201, 442-6856

Hero's Welcome General Store, 3537 U.S. Route 2, North Hero 05474, 372-4161

Hinesburg General Store, 14312 Vermont Route 116, Hinesburg 05461, 482-2820

Historic Craftsbury General Store, 118 South Craftsbury Road, Craftsbury 05826, 586-2893

*H.N. Williams Store, Dorset 05251, 867-5353

Hog Island Market, 172 Lakewood Drive, Swanton 05488, 868-5865

Hubbard's General Store, Vermont Route 125, Hancock 05748, 767-9030

Hyde Park Village Market, Hyde Park 05655, 888-5335

Irasville Country Store, 5130 Main Street, Waitsfield 05673, 496-5400

Isle La Motte Country Store, 68 School Street, Isle La Motte 05463, 928-3033

Jacksonville General Store, 3054 Vermont Route 100, Jacksonville 05342, 368-2822

Jacob & Sons Market, 16 Park Street, Underhill 05489, 899-2511

Jake's South Street Market, 181 South Street, Springfield 05156, 885-5488

Jamaica Country Market, Jamaica 05343, 874-4151

Jaques Country Store, 2246 Main Road, Huntington 05462, 434-8650

Jay's Country Store, Vermont Route 242, North Troy 05859, 988-4040

*Jericho Center Country Store, 25 Jericho Center Road, Jericho 05465, 899-3313

Jericho General Store, Vermont Route 15, Jericho 05465, 899-4661

Jerusalem Corners Country Store, 1858 Vermont Route 17, Bristol 05443, 453-4056

J.J. Hapgood Village Market, Peru 05152, 824-5911

JNB General Store, 26 The Common, Chester 05143, 875-5624

Joe's Pond Country Store, 979 West Shore Road, West Danville 05873, 684-3630

Jolley's Store, 341 Vermont Route 15, Jericho 05465, 899-2507

*Kamuda's Country Store, Pittsford 05763, 483-2361

Keeler's Bay Variety, 500 U.S. Route 2, South Hero 05486, 372-4465

Keith's Country Store, U.S. Route 7, Pittsford 05763, 483-6489

Ken's Country Store, Wilder 05088, 295-2110

Kerrigan's Market, 4080 U.S. Route 5, West Burke 05871, 467-8800

Lackey's Variety Store, Main Street, Stowe 05672, 253-7624

Lake Hortonia General Store, 303 Vermont Route 144, Hubbardton 05760, 273-2577

Lake Parker Country Store, Main Street, West Glover 05875, 525-6985

Lakeview General Store, Vermont Route 114, Averill 05901, 822-5570

Lamarche Albany Market, Albany 05820, 755-6810

Lantman's IGA, Hinesburg 05461, 482-2361

Lawson's Store, 40 Church Hill Road, Websterville 05678, 476-7661

Leicester General Store, 1620 U.S. Route 7, Brandon 05733, 247-4148

Lincoln General Store, 17 East River Road, Lincoln 05443, 453-2981

Lisai's Chester Market, 92 Atkinson Street, Chester 05143, 875-4715

Little Country Store, 2280 Memorial Drive, St. Johnsbury 05819, 748-1661

Lowell General Store, 3042 Vermont Route 100, Lowell 05847, 744-6858

Lucier Store, 4167 Vermont Route 105, Newport Center 05857, 334-8056

Ludlow Country Store, 471 Vermont Route 103 South, Ludlow 05149, 228-8934

Lunenburg Variety, Lunenburg 05906, 892-1147

*Machs' General Store, 18 School Street, Pawlet 05761, 325-3405

Main Street Cash Market, 162 North Main Street, West Rutland 05777, 438-9880

Maple Corner Store, 31 West County Road, Calais 05648, 229-4329

Martin's General Store, 2934 U.S. Route 7, Highgate Springs 05460, 868-4459

Maurais General Store, 22 River Road, Canaan 05903, 266-3900

Mayhew's Corner Store, 1 River Street, Richford 05476, 848-3819

*Mendon Country Store, 39 U.S. Route 4, Mendon 05701, 773-4025

Messier's General Store, 29 Vermont Route 14 South, East Randolph 05041, 728-5750

Middlesex Country Store, 903 U.S. Route 2, Montpelier 05602, 229-4317

Mike & Tammy's Main Street Market, 2170 Vermont Route 11, Londonderry 05148

Mike's Market, Main Street, Island Pond 05846, 723-4747

Mike's Store, Vermont Route 5, Hartland 05048, 436-3244

Minor's Country Store, 874 Main Street, Fairfax 05454, 849-6838

Monkton General Store, 231 Montkton Road #A, Bristol 05443, 453-2385

Moretown General Store, Vermont Route 100B, Moretown 05661, 496-6580

*Morgan Country Store, Morgan 05853, 895-2726

Mountain Paul's General Store, Main Street, Putney 05346, 387-4446

*Newbury Village Store, Main Street, Newbury 05051, 866-5681

*Newfane Market, Newfane 05345, 365-7775

Newport Center Market, Vermont Route 105, Newport 05855, 334-3077

Nichols Store, Main Street, Danby 05739, 293-5154

Noe Place, 106 Vermont Route 30, Jamaica 05353, 874-4831

*Northern Exposure Country Store, Vermont Route 5A, Orleans 0586, 525-3789

North Tunbridge General Store, Vermont Route 110, Tunbridge 05077, 889-3312

Norton Country Store, 564 Vermont Route 114, Norton 05907, 822-5511

Notchbrook General Store, 4968 Mountain Road, Stowe 05672, 253-9448

Old Brick Store, 290 Ferry Road, Charlotte 05445, 425-2421

Original General Store, Vermont Route 100, Pittsfield 05762, 746-8888

Orleans General Store, 72 Main Street, Orleans 05860, 754-6365

Ottauquechee Country Store, 3699 Woodstock Road, White River Junction 05001, 295-7563

*Panton General Store, 3074 Jersey Street, Panton 05491, 475-2431

Peacham Store, 641 Bailey-Hazen Road, Peacham 05862, 592-3310

Plainfield Red Store, U.S. Route 2, Plainfield 05667, 454-7886

Plymouth Country Store, Plymouth 05056, 672-3326

Poultney Market & Spirits, 206 Main Street, Poultney 05764, 287-5732

*Powers Market, Lincoln Square, Nine Main Street, North Bennington 05257, 442-6821

Pratt's Store, 2504 Vermont Route 22A, Bridport 05734, 758-2323

Putney General Store, Main Street, Putney 05346, 387-5842

Ray's Meat & Grocery Market, 100 Park Avenue, Irasburg 05845, 754-6591

Reading Country Store, Reading 05062, 484-7700

Readsboro General Store, Main Street, Readsboro 05350, 423-5477

Richmond Corner Market, 10 East Main Street, Richmond 05477, 434-2519

Rick & Tina's Country Store, Vermont Route 14, Hartford 05047, 295-3083

*Ripton Country Store, Ripton 05766, 388-7328

Riverbend Country Store, North Montpelier 05666, 454-7101

Robinson Olde Country Store, 657 Village Road East, Corinth 05039, 439-6100

*Roxbury Country Store, 1616 Roxbury Road, Roxbury 05669, 485-8857

Saxtons River Village Market, Saxtons River 05154, 869-2266

Shaftsbury Country Store, Shaftsbury 05262, 447-8729

Sharon Trading Post, Sharon 05065, 763-7404

Shaw's General Store, Main Street, Stowe 05672, 253-4040

Sheldon Creek Market, 472 Crowe Hill Road, Sheldon 05483, 933-4783

Sherman's Store, West Rupert 05768, 394-7820

Singleton's Store, 356 Main Street, Proctorsville 05153, 226-7666

Smith's Grocery, 767 Main Street, Greensboro Bend 05842, 533-2631

Snow's Market, Vermont Route 100, Stowe 05672, 253-8043

*Snowsville General Store, Randolph 05060, 728-5252

South Newfane General Store, 397 Dover Road, South Newfane 05351, 348-7133

*South Woodstock Country Store, South Woodstock 05071, 457-3050

Spear's Corner Store, 20 Jackson Hill Road, Charlotte 05445, 425-4444

Stafford's Country Store, Main Street, Stowe 05672, 253-7361

Starksboro Country Store, Starksboro 05487, 453-7760

Stevens' Country Store, Main Street, Washington 05675, 883-2220

Sunrise General Store, 44 U.S. Route 4, Bridgewater Corners 05035, 422-3372

Sylvester's Market, 1012 Mountain Road, Montgomery Center 05471, 326-4561

*Taftsville Country Store, Taftsville 05073, 457-1135

Tallman's Store, Main Street, Belvidere 05442, 644-2751

Teago General Store, Barnard Stage Road, North Pomfret 05053, 457-1626

Ted's Market, Cross Street, Island Pond 05846, 723-4334

Tewksbury's Corner Store, Main Street, Randolph 05060, 728-5620

Troy Country Store, 6561 Vermont Route 100, Troy 05868, 744-6146

Troy General Store, Vermont Route 100, Troy 05868, 744-2200

Tyson Village Store, 1786 Vermont Route 100 North, Ludlow 05149, 228-2284

Underhill Country Store, Underhill Center 05490, 899-4056

Upham's Store, Chelsea 05038, 685-3085

Vermont Energy Market, U.S. Route 7, Ferrisburgh 05456, 877-6714

Vermont General Store, 16 Elm Street, Woodstock 05091, 457-3035

Village Corner Store, 26 Main Street, Bristol 05443, 453-2216

Village Green Market, 48 Town Hill Road, New Haven 05472, 453-2163

*Village Grocery & Deli, 4348 Main Street, Waitsfield 05673, 496-4477

Village Pantry du Logis, 1 Main Street, South Londonderry 05155, 824-9800

Village Store, 304 Vermont Route 110, Tunbridge 05077, 889-9888

*Waits River General Store, West Topsham 05086, 439-5360

Walden General Store, Vermont Route 15, West Danville 05873, 563-3102

*Wardsboro Country Store, Wardsboro 05355, 896-6411

*Warren Store, Warren 05674, 496-3864

Watroba's General Store, 2265 Forest Dale Road, Brandon 05733, 247-3794

*Wayside Country Store, West Arlington 05250, 375-2792

Wells Country Store, 150 Vermont Route 30, Wells 05774, 645-0332

West Addison General Store, Vergennes 05491, 759-2071

West Charleston Corner Store, Vermont Route 105, West Charleston 05872, 895-4300

Westfield General Store, Westfield 05874, 744-2223

West Hartford Village Store, West Hartford 05084, 280-1708

Weston Village Store, Weston 05161, 824-5477

West Street Corner Market, 36 West Street, Proctor 05765, 459-3322

West Topsham Country Store, 486 Vermont Route 25, West Topsham 05086, 439-6400

West Wardsboro Market, 47 Cross Road, West Wardsboro 05359, 896-6666

Wheelock Village Store, 1311 Vermont Route 122, Wheelock 05851, 626-8030

Whiting Country Store, 39 South Main Street, Whiting 05778, 623-6558

Whitingham Country Store, Vermont Route 100, Whitingham 05361, 368-2797

*Willey's Store, Main Road, Greensboro 05841, 533-2621

Williamsville General Store, 1 Main Street, Williamsville 05362, 348-7300

*Will's Store, Main Street, Chelsea 05038, 685-3368

Wing's Supermarket, Main Street, Fairlee 05045, 333-9790

Winhall Market, Bondville 05340, 297-1933

Wolcott Store, Wolcott 05680, 888-3972

Woodbury Village Store, Vermont Route 14, Woodbury 05681, 472-3500

Wooden Barrel Country Store, 231 Chittenden Road, Chittenden 05737, 775-5355

BIBLIOGRAPHY AND SOURCES

Albers, Jan. *Hands on the Land: A History of the Vermont Landscape.* Rutland, VT: Orton Family Foundation, 2000.

Allen, Robert Willis. *Marching On! John Brown's Ghost from the Civil War to Civil Rights.* Northfield, VT: Northfield News & Printery, 2000.

Beck, Jane C. *The General Store in Vermont: An Oral History.* Middlebury, VT: Vermont Folklife Center, 1988.

Budbill, David. *Judevine* (rev. ed.). White River Junction, VT: Chelsea Green Publishing, 1999.

Burnham, Henry. *Brattleboro, Windham Country, Vermont: Early History.* Brattleboro, VT: D. Leonard, 1880.

Carleton, Hiram. *Genealogical and Family History of the State of Vermont.* New York: Lewis Publishing Company, 1903.

Carson, Gerald. *The Old Country Store.* New York: Oxford University Press, 1954.

Conger, Beach, MD. *Bag Balm and Duct Tape: Tales of a Vermont Doctor.* New York: Ballantine Books, 1988.

Coolidge, Calvin. *The Autobiography of Calvin Coolidge.* New York: Cosmopolitan Book Corporation, 1929.

Dean, Howard B. Inaugural Address, January 7, 1993.

Duffy, John J., et al., eds. *The Vermont Encyclopedia.* Burlington: University of Vermont Press, 2003.

E-mail correspondence with Gary Lord, Barbara Parker, Bill Keogh and William Harris.

Faillace, Linda. *Mad Sheep: The True Story Behind the USDA's War on a Family Farm.* White River Junction, VT: Chelsea Green Publishing, 2006.

Fuller, Edmund. *Successful Calamity: A Writer's Follies on a Vermont Farm.* New York: Random House, 1966.

Gazetteer and Business Directory of Chittenden County, 1883.

Gove, Bill. *Sky Route to the Quarries: History of the Barre Railroad.* Barre, VT: Quarry View Publishing, 2004.

Guide to the Appalachian Trail in New Hampshire and Vermont. Harpers Ferry, WV: Appalachian Trail Conference, 1968.

Hard, Walter. *A Mountain Township.* New York: Stephen Daye Press, 1950.

Hemenway, Abby Maria. *The Vermont Historical Gazetteer: A Magazine Embracing a History of Each Town, Civil, Ecclesiastical, Biographical and Military.* Burlington, VT: Miss A.M. Hemenway, 1871.

Interviews transcribed by H.N. Williams as told by his grandmother; and by Jon St. Amour as told by his mother-in-law, Corinne Wilder Thompson.

Interviews with Jireh Billings, Charlotte Downes, Al Floyd, Jan Floyd, Jay Hathaway, George Hayes, Jane Hastings Larrabee, Chief Lone Cloud, Bill MacDonald, Andy Mégroz, John Rehlen, Ray Smith, Jon St. Amour, Doug Tschorn, Nancy Tschorn and Charlie Wilson.

Jones, Robert C. *Railroads of Vermont: A Pictorial.* Shelburne, VT: New England Press, 1994.

Kirkpatrick, Frank. *How to Run a Country Store.* Pownal, VT: Storey Communications, 1986.

Knapp, Ward. *A History of Waterbury.* N.p., 1987.

Lovejoy, Evelyn M. Wood. *History of Royalton, Vermont, with Family Genealogies 1769–1911.* Burlington, VT: Free Press Printing Company, 1911.

Mellin, Jeanne. *The Morgan Horse.* Brattleboro, VT: The Stephen Green Press, 1961.

Morrissey, Charles T. *Vermont: A History.* New York: W.W. Norton, 1981.

Northfield Town History Committee. *Green Mountain Heritage: The Chronicle of Northfield, Vermont.* Canaan, NH: Phoenix Publishing, 1974.

Notes from interviews with Long Trail end-to-ender Stevie Balch, storekeeper Billy Brownlee of H.N. Williams and the employees of Barnard General Store.

Perazzo, Peggy B. "Stone Quarries and Beyond." quarriesandbeyond.org, 2007.

Proctor, Mortimer R. Inaugural Address, January 4, 1945.

Rogers, Barbara Radcliffe, and Stillman Rogers. *Off the Beaten Path: Vermont.* Guilford, CT: Insiders' Guide, 2007.

Rogers, Stillman D., and Barbara Radcliffe Rogers. *Country Towns of Vermont: Charming Small Towns and Villages to Explore.* Chicago: Country Roads Press, 1999.

Sherman, Joe. *Fast Lane on a Dirt Road: A Contemporary History of Vermont.* White River Junction, VT: Chelsea Green Publishing, 2000.

Smith, Charles M. Inaugural Address, January 10, 1935.

Thompson, Linnea H. *A Place of Memory: F.H. Gillingham & Sons, Woodstock, Vermont.* Woodstock, VT: Frank Henry Publishing, 2004.

Thompson, Zadock. *History of Vermont, Natural, Civil, and Statistical.* Burlington, VT: Chauncey Goodrich, 1842.

Thurber, Lois K., and Ann Russette, comps. *Panton—Past and Present; Condensed History of the Town of Panton, Vermont,*

1761–1991. Panton, VT: William and Alberta Kent, 1991.

Tree, Christina, and Diane E. Foulds. *Vermont: An Explorer's Guide.* Woodstock, VT: The Countryman Press, 2006.

Tschorn, Nancy. *Wayside Country Stories.* West Arlington, VT: Nancy Tschorn, pub., 2004.

Two Hundred Vermonters. *Rural Vermont: A Program for the Future.* Burlington: The Vermont Commission on Country Life, 1931.

U.S. Department of Commerce. Current Population Reports, February 12, 1963. Estimates of Illiteracy by States, 1900–60.

Wills, William H. Inaugural Address, January 9, 1941.

Wood, Frederic J. *The Turnpikes of New England and Evolution of the Same Through England, Virginia, and Maryland.* Boston: Marshall Jones Company, 1919.

INDEX

The tour guide is not indexed. Please refer to the beginning of each tour for its towns and stores.